AF713290

SUPERVISORY AND LEADERSHIP SKILLS IN THE MODERN LAW PRACTICE

NITA Editorial Board

Thomas F. Geraghty, Chair
Northwestern University School of Law

Michael H. Ginsberg
Jones Day

Jo Ann Harris
Pace University School of Law

Michael A. Kelly
Walkup, Melodia, Kelly, Wecht & Schoenberger

Robert G. Krupka
Kirkland & Ellis

Anthony J. Bocchino, Editor in Chief
Temple University Beasley School of Law

Zelda Harris, Associate Editor
University of Arizona College of Law

SUPERVISORY AND LEADERSHIP SKILLS IN THE MODERN LAW PRACTICE

Creating a Learning Organization

PAUL J. ZWIER

NITA

© 2006 by the National Institute for Trial Advocacy

All rights reserved. No part of this work may be reproduced or transmitted in any form or by any means, electronic or mechanical, including photocopying and recording, or by any information storage or retrieval system without the prior written approval of the National Institute for Trial Advocacy unless such copying is expressly permitted by federal copyright law. Address inquiries to:

Reprint Permission
National Institute for Trial Advocacy
361 Centennial Parkway, Suite 220
Louisville, CO 80027
Phone: (800) 225-6482
Fax: (720) 890-7069
www.nita.org

Library of Congress Cataloging-in-Publication Data
Zwier, Paul J., 1954–
Supervisory and leadership skills in the modern law practice : creating a learning organization / Paul J. Zwier.
p. cm.
ISBN-13: 978-1-55681-991-9 (pbk.)
ISBN-10: 1-55681-991-9 (pbk.)
1. Law offices—United States. 2. Practice of law—United States.
3. Leadership—United States. I. Title.
KF318.Z88 2006
340.068—dc22
2006034779

FBA: 0991
First printing 2006

Printed in the United States of America

CONTENTS

FOREWORD

Historically, lawyers learned the skills of their profession by observing and assisting senior lawyers. Training and supervision were incidental and implicit: "Do as I do." Mentoring was the glue that bound the profession together. Over years of working together and discussing client issues, lawyers developed professional and personal bonds. Senior lawyers invested their time in the development of the next generation.

The legal profession has changed. Now, lawyers feel pressure for billable hours, profitability, and competitive demands to provide quality client service efficiently. Unquestionably, the profession has become a business. To some, mentoring seems like a quaint but impractical anachronism. Who has the time?

However, investing time in training junior colleagues is still something that busy and successful lawyers should do—not only for the sake of our profession, but because it is in the short-term and long-term self-interest of the senior lawyer. In a law-practice environment, which is a learning organization, everyone learns—and everyone teaches. When everyone is engaged in teaching and learning, clients receive the best service, talented professionals are retained and motivated, and desired profitability is maintained.

Section I provides specific tools that the busy supervising lawyer can employ immediately to increase her effectiveness in guiding junior lawyers, delegating projects, and giving efficient performance feedback. Like any other professional acquiring expertise, a junior lawyer goes through stages of developing competence and an awareness of what competence requires. An effective supervisor takes into account the junior lawyer's stage of development when delegating tasks and communicating feedback. Delegating assignments effectively and efficiently requires a mutual dedication to listening. The supervising lawyer can adopt certain specific precautions to ensure that the supervisee really understands the assignment, thus avoiding delay, expensive write-offs, and a disappointing professional failure for the supervisee. Similarly, delivering efficient performance feedback can improve client service and accelerate the supervisee's acquisition of expertise. By applying the NITA critique model, which emphasizes specificity in improving future performance, a supervisor can maximize the learning value of her feedback with minimal investment of her professional time. These time-efficient tools for delegation and feedback can assist a law-practice group in becoming a learning organization while maintaining profitability and client service. Senior lawyers who are alert to the teaching opportunities that arise in the course of managing a case or a project can structure their team's internal communications so that the higher level functions of management and strategy become visible to supervisees.

Section II discusses how the same supervisory skills of listening well and communicating clearly can form the basis for developing leadership skills within law organizations. We explore more broadly methods by which a law-practice group can facilitate the development of its lawyers, not only in their professional expertise but in becoming mentors and leaders within the organization. When a law-practice group seeks to promote the mentoring of junior lawyers, there are certain practices to adopt—and to avoid—to optimize the mentoring experience for both the mentors and the mentees. The most challenging parts of the practice of law—dealing with mistakes, handling a difficult client, recognizing and addressing ethical issues—are taught and learned when senior lawyers model solutions in a context where junior lawyers can share in arriving at a solution.

PREFACE

Teaching Supervisory Skills Is Essential in the Modern Law Firm

Why should a senior lawyer bother to take the time to train and give feedback to the lawyers who work for him or her at the firm? After all, what busy, successful expert litigator or deal maker actually has the time to teach junior lawyers how to practice law? If an associate fails to do a good job on a project, just get someone else. If you are in a small firm and you can't avoid working with the underperforming associate, fire the offender and next time make sure you hire someone with the requisite experience and skills.

There are two answers to the question of why to take the time to supervise. First, professionalism and professional responsibility require it. Second, in law firms—large and small—and for-profit enterprises with in-house legal departments, it is in the senior lawyer's economic interest to train and to give feedback. In not-for-profit and government law organizations, the institution and its client base are best served by well-trained and productive junior lawyers.

PROFESSIONALISM

The Report of the Professionalism Committee of the ABA Section of Legal Education and Admissions to the Bar reaffirmed that the practice of law is more than a business: it is a learned profession. A profession is an occupation that requires entrants to show dedication to the ideals and practice associated with a learned calling. The report quoted Roscoe Pound's definition of the essence of professionalism: "pursuing a learned art as a common calling in the spirit of public service." [1]

The report expanded on Pound's definition by describing the commitment to training required in the practice of law and urging firms to maintain the competence of its members after graduation and passing the bar. In particular, the report made the following recommendation:

> Practicing lawyers must become acutely aware of the need to nurture and to renew their professionalism ideals on a continuing basis, always aspiring to maintain the highest standards of the lawyer-statesman paradigm. Lawyers should be willing to share their knowledge and experience through mentoring and teach other lawyers by participating in informal and formal mentoring programs and continuing education programs: and they should welcome the opportunity to participate in pro bono programs, non-partisan law reform activities and other programs that promote and enhance professionalism among lawyers. Practicing lawyers also need to do a better job developing in themselves and in their law firms a client-centered mentality where the expectations

> and objectives of the clients and the human relations aspects of the lawyer-client relationship, rather than the potential legal fees in a particular matter, are the principal focus.
>
> ...It is particularly important to the profession for senior lawyers to help the neophyte lawyers to learn how to deal with the extreme pressures placed on their time. How should a lawyer learn to balance billing and other professional time pressures with family obligations, or the need to be expert and efficient with the call to public service, or the desire to win for the client with the need to advise the client against the lawyer's self interest? The help and teaching of the experienced practitioner is vital to professional growth and development. Moreover, competent representation is the first principle of professional responsibility to clients and the legal system. Law firms and senior lawyers in all forms of practice have a professional responsibility duty to insure the competence of the junior lawyers they supervise.[2]

In other words, teaching and mentoring is more than simply the right thing to do, for doing the right thing can have its own rewards. Something more than nostalgia causes senior lawyers to look back on their careers and to value highly the teaching and learning relationships they established with associates and colleagues. Mentoring and teaching may be one of the most important lasting contributions that lawyers make to society and the profession. In supervisory-skills training programs over the past ten years, lawyers have given hundreds of accounts of how valuable and meaningful teaching and learning relationships have been to them as young lawyers. Judges and their clerks, law professors and their students, expert lawyers and their junior colleagues, all describe how these relationships have created meaning and provided fulfillment in the practice of law. Mentoring, whether it be on an ongoing one-on-one basis between a senior and junior lawyer or episodically in the course of client representation, provides support, encouragement, and tough love and inspires the young professional to acquire excellence and efficiency. Teaching and learning in an institution also encourage personal growth beyond the demands of a particular case or project by providing tips on how to navigate firm politics, how to maintain balance in family and community life, and how to find others to mentor so that the cycle of giving back to the rofession continues.

ECONOMICS AND INSTITUTIONAL EFFICIENCY

It is in the economic self-interest of a senior lawyer to have the support of well-trained junior lawyers. Training improves morale, provides meaning, facilitates the gaining of expertise, and accelerates advancement. This in turn allows the junior lawyer to attain higher billing rates more quickly, thereby improving profitability. In firms and other legal organizations, training demonstrates to junior lawyers that the organization values their contribution, which in turn improves retention. Training also improves client service by creating a learning environment that encourages entrepreneurship and creativity. Retaining creative employees allows the firm to remain responsive to client concerns.

The environment in which law firms operate has changed significantly in the past twenty-five years.[3] Just look at the numbers. Table 1, below, lists the top ten law firms by gross revenues.[4]

Table 1. Firm Rank By Gross Revenues

2004	*2005*		*Gross Rev.*
1	1	Skadden	$1,610,000,000
2	3	Latham & Watkins	$1,412,500,000
3	2	Baker & McKenzie	$1,352,000,000
4	4	Jones Day	$1,285,000,000
5	5	Sidley Austin	$1,124,000,000
6	6	White & Case	$1,046,000,000
7	8	Weil, Gotshal	$1,016,500,000
8	7	Mayer, Brown	$980,000,000
9	9	Kirkland & Ellis	$970,000,000
10	25	Piper Rudnick	$890,500,000

Next, look at the growth in the numbers of lawyers in some of the largest firms:

Firms: Selected Major U.S Firms Growth	*Number of Lawyers 1983*	*Number of Lawyers 2006 from firm web page*
Skadden, Arps, Slate, Meagher & Flom	275	1750
Shearman & Sterling	340	1000

Davis Polk & Wardell	251	600
Baker & McKenzie	622	3000
Sidley & Austin	308	1600
Jones Day	301	2200
Vinson & Elkins	318	700
Gibson, Dunn & Crutcher	278	800
Latham & Watkins	183	1800[5]

The economic causes of such growth come from both the supply side and the demand side of the economic equation.

The trend was first noted in the early 1990s. Robert Nelson, in his book review of the *Tournament of Lawyers: The Transformation of the Big Law Firm* summarizes as follows the changes studied by Marc Galanter and Thomas Palay[6]:

> Moreover, in various ways law firms began to modify the traditional partner-associate pyramid. They added large numbers of paralegals to perform tasks previously done by associates. Some firms began to experiment anew with permanent associates or to hire non-tenure track lawyers, who were paid lower salaries than other associates and who were not eligible for partnership. Many firms instituted two-tier partnerships that created a layer of salaried, non-equity partners below the stratum of full partners. Firms also began to lengthen the number of years required before admission to the partnership, from six or seven years to eight or nine years. There are preliminary indications that the proportion of associates

> promoted to partner, after rising somewhat during the high growth years of the seventies and early eighties, has begun to decline. Heightened insecurity has also begun to affect the upper levels of firms. With increasing frequency firms are dismissing or "departnerizing" partners who do not achieve levels of performance and profitability expected by firm leaders.[7]

The pressures on law-firm economics have come from a number of different sources, but each of these pressures points in the same direction: It is essential to the future of law firms to invest in attorney training, in particular focusing on supervisory skills and effectively managing the work of providing quality legal services to increasingly discerning clients. The same is true in not-for-profit and governmental institutions where budgetary restraints prevent expansion of offices, resulting in the need for junior lawyers to be as efficient and expert as possible, as soon as possible.

Law-school education does not provide supervisory skills training, and, for the most part, such skills are passed down from generation to generation only by imitation. Often such supervision consists only of unexplained refusal to give more work to the underperforming lawyer, or, worse, angry words communicating personal judgments about one's abilities but providing no specific suggestions for improvement. Sometimes surviving and getting along within a firm seems to be based less on merit and more on the economic requirements or the predilections and biases of senior supervisors.

A. New Challenges to the Traditional Law-Firm Model

Law-firm economics, at its core, is not complex. Law firms—big and small—are able to operate successfully if they can simultaneously do two related things. First, the firm must generate quality legal work for clients who understand the value of the work and are therefore willing to pay for it, thus generating revenues. Second, the firm must attract and retain talented lawyers by offering them competitive compensation and by otherwise motivating them. If revenues and profits are high enough, both partners and non-partners will receive compensation sufficient to retain them.

However, this model of law-firm economics has been under significant pressure in the last decade from diverse sources: external competition, client demands, and the changing demographics of what motivates young professionals. Law firms now compete not only with other law firms, but with other businesses—not only for client business but also for talent. For example, accounting firms are winning business away from law firms in areas such as tax and corporate transactions. Obviously, when another law firm, an accounting firm, or an investment banking firm provides services to a client or a potential client, it results in a loss of billable hours and a consequent loss of revenue for the firm who lost out on the business. Solving this problem of lost revenue by increasing billing rates is probably short sighted, as it will likely alienate some of the remaining clients, exacerbating the problem. The better solution is to maintain the billable hours by replacing the lost work with other work, which requires maintaining excellent client relationships and work quality. That in turn requires retaining and motivating the strongest performers.

On the other side of the revenue/expense equation, competition for talent can increase law-firm expenses substantially. In the late 1990s, law firms saw a number of their talented associates and the brightest law students recruited away to technology companies and investment banking firms that could offer higher starting salaries and/or the allure of pre-IPO stock options. As a result, all the largest law firms across the country dramatically increased their starting salaries. Many other firms also made upward salary adjustments to remain competitive in the recruiting market. Brand-new law graduates who had never written a brief, argued a motion, or laid eyes on a client, were commanding compensation packages running well into six figures. The sudden significant jump in expenses meant that the firm's profits, and therefore partner compensation, would take an equally sudden and significant drop. Many firms reacted by increasing billing rates and expectations for associate billable hours. This in turn generated pushback from clients who objected to higher rates, as well as dissatisfaction from associates who were disenchanted with the idea of billing yet more hours.

Clients of large law firms are generally sophisticated consumers of legal resources who know the value of the services they receive. Many are willing to take their business to another firm, even if they are receiving quality service, if they feel that the price is too high. Clients may draw the line on billing rates, or they may impose conditions on how the work is to be done: for example, limiting attendance at deposition or hearing to only one lawyer, or limiting the number of lawyers with higher billing rates who may work on a matter. Some clients decline to allow a firm to staff their matter with any lawyer having fewer than three or four years of experience, reasoning that they do not want the firm to be charging them for training at hundreds of dollars per hour. Thus, client demands can proscribe, or at least discourage, the traditional learning vehicle of bringing along a neophyte for the purpose of "learning by watching" how the senior lawyer conducts business.

In addition to these competitive pressures and client demands, law firms are finding that a basic premise of the law-firm model concerning the motivations of young lawyers is becoming increasingly out-of-date. Traditionally, bright young lawyers were willing to be apprenticed for years, performing tedious tasks and deferring any role in the more creative aspects of their cases or transactions. However, the newer generations of law graduates are not so patient. Lawyers of the baby-boom generation, today's senior partners, expected to work their way up the ladder, having watched as their parents often had only one employer for their entire career. Younger lawyers in the post-boomer generation, known as "Generation X," born between 1965 and 1977 came of age during the economic crash of the late 1980s and recession of the early 1990s. They more often had two working parents who changed jobs several times, and they came to expect more responsibility sooner. If asked to choose between success and integrity, fully half would choose success. The next generation, known as "Generation 2001" and born after 1978, expects to be given responsible and creative work right away. Generally they are more motivated by having idealistic and committed coworkers than by the prospect of a remote financial reward.[8] The traditional partner/associate model premised on years of deferred gratification, both financially and in terms of having responsible and creative work, simply does not motivate the younger law-school graduates in the same way it motivated today's senior partners.

However, retaining junior lawyers by providing them with more responsibility and creative work can run counter to what clients demand. Obviously, client service precludes putting bright though inexperienced lawyers in positions of major responsibility. The value that clients expect in legal advice is composed more from wisdom than intelligence. Clients are more willing to pay a very high billing rate to get fifteen minutes of advice from a senior partner than to pay for several hours of research by a law-school graduate. When clients are unwilling to pay for a junior lawyer to observe a seasoned lawyer in deposition or in court or to pay for inexperienced lawyers to have any role at all in their matters, it becomes even more difficult for firms to provide the challenging work that younger lawyers are increasingly expecting and to develop the expertise that optimal client service requires. As a result, many firms have cut back on the hiring of law-school graduates and shifted the recruiting focus to more senior lateral hires with experience both in practicing law and in supervising others.

The challenge for today's legal institutions is to build a

learning organization that engages these new generations of lawyers. Modern law supervisors must be willing to supervise in a way other than the way they were supervised to retain the best and the brightest of the twenty-first century.

B. The Focus on Retention of Experienced Non-Partner Lawyers

Each of these recent challenges facing law firms seems to point in the same direction: firms need more experienced non-partner lawyers who are fully engaged in their practices. They must not only be skilled; they must be fully engaged in their work and happily so. Clients are willing to pay for the services of lawyers they perceive are already trained and can work efficiently enough to justify their high billing rates. When junior lawyers are properly supervised, trained, and mentored, the quality of work produced remains high, and the firm is able to keep the client in the face of external competition. In addition, the firm is able to retain the junior lawyer in the face of his or her professional alternatives.

Moreover, the experienced non-partner is the most profitable employee the firm can hire. Untrained junior lawyers will spend more time on non-billable activities and will be more inefficient, requiring that some of their time recorded as billable is written off. At least two Midwest law firms have analyzed their operations to confirm that their associates do not become profitable to the firm (i.e., generate more revenue than their compensation and pro rata allocation of overhead) until an associate's third or fourth year. In other words, the costs associated with the new lawyer exceed the revenue she generates for the first three or four years of practice. To the extent that this inflection point of profitability can be reached more quickly, the law firm will benefit. Similarly, in not-for-profit and governmental practice, the more quickly junior lawyers achieve competence, the more quickly they provide quality and efficient client service.

Given that lawyers are most profitable for the firm during the period after they have acquired a certain level of experience and before they become partners, it is not surprising that law firms would want to maximize that period. Accordingly, many firms have extended the expected track for partnership consideration. One major New York firm, for example, now has a partnership track of fourteen years. In addition, many firms have created new classes of employees, referred to as counsel or non-equity partners, to increase retention of these profitable non-partners by giving them recognition of their professional progress while still reserving (in some cases, indefinitely) the sharing of profits to a smaller group of equity partners.[9]

However, lengthening the partnership track can succeed in maximizing profits only if the experienced non-partners remain with the firm. Retention is critical, and extending the time for partnership consideration presents obvious risks to the institution. Making reward or recognition more remote will certainly demotivate some talented individuals, who may decide to leave the firm because they can obtain reward or recognition sooner elsewhere. Furthermore, other talented individuals may not be motivated by partnership, sufficiently or at all, to invest years acquiring expertise in the traditional way. In either of these cases, the firm will see talented and profitable employees walk out the door.

Perhaps for this reason, other firms have directed their efforts to lengthen the period of maximum productivity by focusing on the other end: i.e., shortening the time it takes a law-school graduate or new hire to function as an experienced lawyer for whom clients feel comfortable paying a high billing rate. For example, one Midwest firm undertook a training program to accelerate the break-even point at which associates generate more revenue than the cost of their compensation and overhead. The firm's goal was to shorten that period from three or four years to eighteen months. To that end, they created a skills inventory for each stage of lawyer development in each area of firm practice, and then provided skills and substantive training programs designed to address the appropriate stage of development. Another multi-city law firm undertook a similar effort to accelerate profitability, as well as to ensure a firm-wide standard of practice, by providing its litigation associates with an integrated learning-by-doing training program. Other major firms have recently placed a renewed emphasis on training, including in one instance the creation of a full-time partnership position dedicated to formal associate training.

By shortening the time to highly profitable "mid-level associate" status, a firm enables its associates to accept more responsibility earlier and thereby justifies a higher billing rate. This also accelerates these associates to a position of delegating work and supervising incoming associates, paralegals, and secretaries, thus placing a premium on early development of supervisory skills.

Some firms believe that investing resources in training associates to accelerate profitability is a waste of money, because many of those associates will leave the firm in any event. Certainly, some associates will leave because they are unable to perform at the required level of proficiency. For these lawyers, there should be in place a well-developed and implemented evaluation process to assist the firm in identifying associates who do not have the ability necessary to become long-term contributors at the firm. But ultimately, the investment in training, and in particular supervisory skills training, will most effectively advance the interdependent goals of generating quality work and retaining talented people to do that work. Given the evolution in what motivates bright people, increasing numbers of young lawyers cannot be retained without an assurance that they will be given responsibility and an opportunity to do creative and innovative work. If they see that their colleagues likewise value a rewarding and challenging work experience, they are more likely to want to stay and to contribute to the firm. Thus, the retention of talented lawyers—which is the key to both short-term profitability and long-term viability—depends on the willingness of law firms to view themselves as learning organizations. These principles apply no matter how big the firm.

These retention issues apply with equal force to not-for-profit and governmental practices. Although not concerned with profitability, these institutions must nevertheless provide efficient and expert service to their clients. Like their law-firm counterparts, junior lawyers in these practice settings expect early responsibility and recognition, and indeed may have been attracted to such positions (and foregone large-firm compensation) for the very purpose of gaining experience. For them, training and the accumulation of expertise (as well as public service) may be a primary motivating factor.

C. The Law Firm as a Learning Organization

Peter Senge, in his book *The Fifth Discipline,* describes the need for today's businesses to be "learning organizations" in order to be able to successfully compete and adapt to the changing needs of its customers.[10] Law firms are businesses, and increasingly large businesses. The largest law firms have grown explosively in the past thirty years. However, growth depends on retention, and talented people will remain and thrive in the organizations that both compensate them competitively and engage them in a learning environment.

The theory of a business as a learning organization is premised on the notion that to survive in a fast-paced global market the business must have its front-line people continually interested in learning and growing.[11] If the organization emphasizes efficiency in the short run, it will sacrifice service and lose employees. If the organization focuses only on its current business and how it can deliver the same product at lower cost, it most likely will not be able to respond if and when the market changes and makes that product obsolete. If, however, the firm's front-line people are continually in a learning mode and are on the lookout for the next new thing, then they can be there to solve problems and to offer new ideas. For example, they can stop drafting real estate investment trusts (REITs) when the business and tax environments change and instead can work on other kinds of securities. They can train their junior lawyers well in the art of trial skills, but can switch modes easily if they find themselves in arbitration or mediation. In addition, firms can teach the "people skills" of interviewing, active listening, planning, and negotiation that transfer easily into other forms of alternative dispute resolution. They can protect and defend, and attack and parry, but they can also facilitate and counsel, and negotiate and mediate.

In a law firm that is a learning organization, everyone learns—and everyone teaches.[12] Partners circulate drafts of their own writing, not just to other partners but also to junior lawyers on the team. Partners perform mock arguments in the office before important hearings, and associates as well as other partners attend, pose questions, and offer input. The goal is not to preserve the fiction that partners are smarter than non-partners; the goal is simply to give the client the best product that the team is capable of producing. By including the junior lawyers in the high-level task of creating the best possible work product, the senior lawyers engage the Generation Xers and Generation 2001ers in the most creative aspects of the practice of law.[13] They also give them the experience of seeing how more seasoned lawyers work in a collaborative environment. Perhaps most significantly, they model how they expect junior lawyers to approach their tasks: to be creative but ruthlessly attentive to detail, to be confident and willing to take risks while remaining open to feedback.

In a law-practice environment in which junior lawyers expect to teach as well as to learn, they are more engaged, and from whatever generation, more motivated. Imagine that an associate tasked to do 200 hours of tedious document review is invited to give a presentation to her work group on how to organize and implement an effective document review. Several things will happen. First, what may have seemed like a gruesome task will now take on a creative aspect. Second, the associate will learn more effectively how to accomplish the task: Anyone who has given a presentation knows that you never learn something as well as when you have to teach it. Third, by teaching others the associate will have an opportunity to contribute something to the institution and experience a sense of responsibility beyond the performance of the client service. The partners will gain an insight they would not otherwise have had about the skill level and talent of the associate: How effectively can this young lawyer see the big picture and communicate it? Finally, the partners will also gain a data point as to this associate's interest level in contributing to the community of the firm—an important subjective element in evaluating the associate's long-term relationship with the firm.

The economic case for taking the time to mentor, supervise, and otherwise create a learning environment is compelling. The pressures of increasing competition and client demands for law firms and the need for efficiency and expertise in all practice settings have not rendered training of junior lawyers obsolete. To the contrary, for just those reasons, training is more important than ever. In particular, training on how to mentor, supervise, delegate, and manage is critical to keep the practice of law economically viable and a realistic choice as a pleasurable and rewarding lifetime occupation.

• SECTION ONE •

Developing Supervisory Skills in the Course of Client Service

Much can be done to create a learning environment when a law firm becomes more aware of the learning opportunities that occur every day in the workplace.[14] Learning and teaching in the law organization start with an identification of the skills required at various levels of development and a commitment to conscious practice of those skills. With a heightened understanding of how the learning needs of its lawyers change depending on the stage in their development of expertise, the firm can create the right structures and right incentives to fit the associates' needs. Whether it means the firm should implement a comprehensive mentoring program (discussed in Chapter 6), or a management program to build teamwork and communications skills, or an efficient feedback system between more- and less-experienced attorneys, the firm can marshal its resources to best fit its needs and the type of environment it wants to create. While mentoring may be the ideal in some situations, some see time constraints as necessitating a feedback system that is more concise and focused. The skills necessary for effective supervision are the same. They can be utilized in a long-term, one-on-one mentoring relationship, or in a one-time suggestion on how to improve in the course of a particular representation involving senior and junior lawyers.

Under any model of supervision, the skills of delegation and effective feedback are fundamental to creating a learning environment among junior and senior lawyers within any legal-practice setting. Essential to both skills is an understanding of the learning stages that lawyers, and all professionals, go through as they seek to gain expertise. Supervisors need skills to deliver feedback in a clear and concise manner. Lawyers working together need to develop a shared language to make delegation and feedback work together to maximize the junior lawyer's attainment of expert legal skills and values, which in turn can be passed on to each succeeding generation of lawyers within the law-practice setting.

· CHAPTER ONE ·

Understanding the Developmental Stages of Expertise

One key to creating a vibrant and effective learning environment at a firm is to provide different types of education tailored to the different stages through which lawyers will advance in gaining expertise. Supervisors can learn much about becoming experts in their supervising skills by looking at what learning psychologists know about gaining expertise in other disciplines, such as music or sports.[15]

When learning psychologists look at the process of gaining expertise across disciplines, they see a number of common features in the development of experts. First, experts note that they had successful experience early on when they attempted the skill. Second, most attribute a lot of their success to a mentor or coach who encouraged their development. Third, each expert seems to have spent a minimum of four hours a day, for approximately ten years, developing their skills. Finally, the "practice" in which they engage is not repetition for repetition's sake, but an intentional practice that breaks down the skill into its component parts. As each component is practiced, the budding expert is able to work intentionally on that aspect of the practice until she can do it automatically and without conscious thought.

Often these experts talk about the encouragement and support they received from parents or teachers when they first took up the skill. From Brooks Robinson to Tiger Woods to Mozart, these experts had early encouragement from someone they admired. Many athletes and musicians also describe a common experience of "getting in the zone," a metaphoric place where they are performing at the very highest level. In "the zone," time seems to slow down. They are not hurried or anxious. They describe an almost out-of-body experience, in which they are thinking ahead about what they will do while they are "automatically" doing something else. They are completely focused. They are not afraid, but are concentrating, often with the use of a mantra that allows them to set aside their surroundings to "get out of the way" of their bodies to allow them to perform as they have practiced.

Expert lawyers describe the same phenomenon. She knew what questions to ask on cross-examination because she was "in the zone," thinking three steps ahead of the witness. Because he had been in the situation so many times before, he was able to anticipate exactly what concerns the bankruptcy trustee would have and knew exactly what to say to alleviate those concerns and secure his position.

To gain expertise, it is essential that the learner receives feedback and instruction tailored to his or her stage of development and to his or her individual learning style. Childhood skill development is instructive here. While parenting is important, maximizing improvement requires, at a particular developmental point, that a non-parent coach design individual objective learning goals and strategies and provide a mix of incentives, positive feedback, and tough love in the right combination.[16]

First, the learning needs to be tailored to the learner's stage of development. Just as it is inappropriate for a young opera singer to attempt certain pieces of music too early, law firms should tailor instruction to fit the needs of the attorneys at their particular stages of development. For example, an inexperienced cross-examiner should not attempt an open-ended question on cross-examination when he is still learning the difference between open-ended and leading questions. While an experienced deal maker might know when to draft a contract provision independent of an existing model from a similar deal, the neophyte is better advised to create the first draft by tracking closely the existing model. At the same time learning must be appropriate to the stage of development, it is also important that the learner be challenged to reach the next level of his or her understanding if he or she is to maintain learning momentum and the incentive to strive for more.

For maximum benefit, the teaching and learning will need to be personalized. There are different strategies that a firm can employ to provide personalized and appropriate education for gaining expertise. A firm can employ techniques of mentoring, coaching, or managing. It can also employ strategies of leadership using training and learning by example. Firms can and do employ some or all of these educational strategies to hasten attainment of expertise and to create a learning environment.

In most organizations, members go through fairly predictable stages of development of their own expertise.[17]

First, there is the *unconscious incompetence* stage. The associate is so green he does not even know when he is showing his incompetence. An inexperienced litigation associate may include an evenhanded bench-memo analysis in his first points and authorities in support of a motion, and while this may have worked well in law school, it is not the advocacy piece that the client wants and the partner is expecting. An inexperienced transactional associate might mislabel the names of the parties in the contract's opening paragraph, or fail to do a search-and-replace edit on a draft to excise the inapplicable portions of the template he is using. Once a "young 'un" has made a blunder, this stage can be marked by the neophyte's fear of failure or drawing further attention to himself on account of that failure. Like an adolescent, he just does not want to be embarrassed and will avoid taking risks.

The unconscious incompetent has very concrete needs. He wants to know how to fill out time sheets, what forms memos should take, to whom he should speak to get supplies, and where to stand in court when conducting a direct examination. This early stage is also characterized by a herd mentality and by risk-averse behavior. As a result, a junior lawyer might limit himself to only the task given him and nothing more. He may not seek out extra work and may not worry about the big-picture questions. He may attend only to protecting himself from standing out or making a mistake.

The second stage is often referred to as *conscious incompetence.* Having learned of his incompetence, the young associate can become hyperconscious and insecure about other things. He now knows how much he has to learn. If appropriately encouraged or born with strength of character, the more self-confident associate will set about the task of learning everything he can about the practice. He is innately intellectually curious or competitive. He now needs not only concrete information about the dos and don'ts of his practice area, but he is also hungry for the more strategic information needed to take on more responsibility. He will start to want to see the big picture, to be able to anticipate the needs of supervisees and the senior supervisor, so that he can be one step ahead and ready to move into the next stage.

The next stage is *conscious competence.* In this stage, the relationship between associate and firm is marked by the associate's productive and efficient service to the firm and supervisees. The associates are still learning and growing, and they need to think consciously about what they are doing and motivate themselves to do it. Their skills are conscious, and they take pride in their accomplishments and the results they obtain. They work long hours and have little time for teaching others. They often believe that it is far easier for them to just do the task at hand by themselves than to take the time to teach someone else. They have the greatest need to delegate and yet the least time to delegate. These lawyers often seek out training on time management and setting priorities. They are interested in leadership issues and firm politics.

Mentoring lawyers in this stage of their development takes less time. By this point, they are developing self-confidence and are less dependent on the senior supervisor for their professional self-worth. They have their own needs to delegate and to supervise more junior lawyers.

Firms should think carefully about how to encourage supervisors to move their supervisees from unconscious incompetence to conscious incompetence to conscious competence. While these supervisees are still not efficient and proficient, their learning curve during the conscious incompetence stage is extraordinary—if they are motivated to learn. It is with this group that the mentor can make a real difference.

For example, a supervisee can learn a great deal by coauthoring an article or teaming up to make a presentation with a supervisor about a cutting-edge problem. In this setting of guided research and team writing and presenting, the supervisor can gauge the supervisee's readiness and understanding of the topic and can provide a safety net when the associate might get in over his head. The conscious incompetent develops the skill of being self-aware and self-reflective. This skill of knowing what you know and what you do not know, and taking steps to learn what you do not know, is foundational for acquiring expertise.

Finally, many senior attorneys sometimes evolve to a stage that can be called *unconscious competence.* This stage is marked by the ease and efficiency with which an attorney practices. One expert also has noted that some supervisors in this stage lose interest in spending long hours in the practice.[18] They are skillful at what they do and can rest on their laurels. Because they now get more satisfaction from pursuing challenges outside the practice, they spend more time on firm management, recruitment of lawyers to the firm, community work, or politics.

These lawyers are prime candidates to be the firm's teachers and mentors. However, this group is often less conscious about how and why they do what they do as practicing lawyers. Their diminished interest in the practice may make them resistant to a teaching role, as Michael Jordan might have little interest in teaching a youngster how to dribble. If inclined to teach at all, these senior lawyers are more likely interested in teaching complex techniques rather than basic skills: for example, complex strategic thinking rather than how to begin a deposition. In training settings, they are often contrarians, inclined to see the contextual nature of the practice that may call for a different approach than the one being taught. This contrarian effect can be mitigated by engaging these lawyers in the training effort: For example, when NITA faculty present an in-house learning-by-doing program on basic skills, the faculty can team with the firm's senior lawyers who teach the advanced or firm-specific applications of the basic skills.

On the other hand, those in the unconscious competence stage who mentor can find it to be an extremely rewarding task. They can inspire and motivate, thus accelerating the young supervisor's learning curve immensely. They can help advance the unconscious incompetent to the conscious incompetent to the consciously competent. The firm can then reach the break-even point of profitability sooner. With greater skills come more effective delegation, higher billing rates, and more time for the senior lawyer to spend on the higher-level tasks. The economic benefits are twofold: attorney turnover before break-even is reduced, and the firm's attorneys become more competent earlier in their careers.

• CHAPTER TWO •

Delegating Assignments Effectively and Efficiently

WHY DELEGATING IS IMPORTANT AND DIFFICULT

Profitability depends on efficiency in delivering legal services. Efficiency, in turn, requires effective delegation.

For a law firm to maximize profits, the legal work must be done by the professional with the billing rate most appropriate for the task at hand. Firm partners need to be able to push work down to the highly leveraged professionals, usually senior associates and often senior paralegals, who have high billing rates relative to their compensation. Sophisticated clients will balk at paying for inefficiency, which notably includes having work done at a billing rate higher than is warranted by the complexity or importance of the work. The habit of some busy lawyers to handle a task themselves, rather than to take the time to delegate, can generate problems once the client reviews the bill. Effective delegation does take time. As discussed earlier, one of the defining characteristics of the consciously competent group is that they have the greatest need to delegate, yet they have the least time and perhaps the least inclination to do so. It does take time to think through how to involve another lawyer in accomplishing the task efficiently and how to explain the task in a reasonably thorough manner.

Unfortunately, delegation is often undertaken without the necessary investment of time: a practice that is, to paraphrase the maxim, minute wise and hour foolish. By the time the busy lawyer realizes that she cannot get it all done herself, or acknowledges that a particular aspect of the project could be more efficiently handled by someone with a lower billing rate, the deadline is often looming. By the time she locates a delegatee and has a moment to sit down with him, she is preoccupied with meeting the deadline and does not focus on the delegation itself. The delegator is often not clear in her own mind—at least when she starts the delegation discussion and perhaps even when it concludes—about exactly what she wants from the delegatee. She gives short shrift to the effort necessary to ensure that the delegatee understands the context of his task, the audience for his written product, or even the precise question(s) he should be answering. A disaster—and a large write-off—is in the making.

When delegation is ineffective, the resulting disaster often takes the following familiar form: The memorandum presented to the delegating attorney, thousands of client-dollars later, bears no resemblance to what the delegator thought she was asking for. The story is well known about a young lawyer who, when asked to research an evidence question, photocopied a hornbook on present-sense impressions and put it on the supervisor's desk, never thinking through the fact situation the delegating attorney needed to address. Many junior lawyers, not given appropriate guidance in the delegation process, write a lengthy treatise without understanding or taking into account the factual context that called for the research. Sometimes the opposite result—equally undesirable—occurs, when the work product consists of a short concise answer that fails to consider analogies or to construct different ways around the general rule, even though the delegator, without specifying, intended that the research provide as much.

Obviously the communication that took place in these delegation processes was faulty. Effective delegation requires both clear thinking of the part of the delegator and successful communication between delegator and delegatee. Since communication is a two-way street, optimizing the delegation process requires consideration of both sides of the communication.

DECONSTRUCTING DELEGATION

One way of examining how senior lawyers delegate is to deconstruct the delegation process by using a listening drill. Each member of the group should think of a work in progress that he would like to delegate to another lawyer. Participants should be paired with colleagues from different parts of the firm: e.g., litigators with transactional supervisors, bankruptcy supervisors with estate planners, appellate supervisors with environmental supervisors. This pairing deprives the delegators of the advantage of the vocabulary they have in common with their practice colleagues, and thereby puts a premium on the delegator's effort to think through exactly what he wants and to communicate it in plain terms.

Each participant will delegate an assignment and will receive an assignment from her partner. The group should expect to use about ten minutes per delegation, or a total of about twenty minutes for the exercise. The group should assume that the delegator is going to take a two-week vacation and, although there are telephones at his destination, he really does not want to be disturbed unless it is absolutely necessary.

This drill has a few rules that make it different from the usual mode of conversation with which the participants are familiar. For that reason, it may be most effective for the facilitator to do a demonstration round, acting as delegatee with a volunteer who will serve as delegator. The rules for the drill are as follows:

Listening Drill

1. No questions
2. Restate what you hear
3. Reflect
4. Repeat restatement and reflection until understanding is confirmed
5. Then, in the real world, ask questions

Rule 1: No questions

Acknowledge that this rule will be very difficult to follow, especially for lawyers who make their living by asking questions and generally believe they are very good at asking questions. The purpose of the rule is to get the delegatee to focus her attention on *just* listening. When the delegatee starts asking questions, she stops getting the information that the delegator wants to give and starts to get only the information she requested. The participant will need to resist his lawyerly instinct to start problem solving. When problem solvers stop listening and start concluding too early, they will often run into trouble (e.g., medical misdiagnosis, a result of failing to learn about all the symptoms). The "No questions" rule does not mean no feedback. The delegatee is allowed to use nonverbal communication (nods, quizzical looks, furrowed brow) or comments such as "Yes" or "I see" to the end of keeping the delegator talking. Points to emphasize to particpants are:

- Delegators are often "works in progress." If they are honest, they are often not clear in their own minds about what help they need, what form it should take, and what priorities should govern the work. Some of this lack of clarity is inherent in the process because it is unknown what the delegatee will find in his research. However, the delegator can succeed in being much clearer if he prepares for the delegation conversation.
- It is often difficult to evaluate how much background and context the delegatee needs.
- Asking questions interrupts the delegator's thought process and may risk showing the delegator that the delegatee is not listening for understanding.

Participants playing the delegator role report how unusual, and generally pleasant, it is to be listened to without interruption.

Rule 2: Restate what you hear

Just because the delegatee is not asking questions does not mean she cannot communicate to the delegator. The delegatee should be directed to interrupt early and often with restatements of what she just heard. She should not simply parrot what she has heard, but should try to restate *in her own words* what she understands. This requires that the listener quiet the problem-solving side of her brain and focus first on the job of listening for understanding. Instead of posing a question, the delegatee might say, "I think I'm with you so far. Let me restate what you've said, and you tell me whether I've got it so far." In other words, the job of the delegator during restatement is to listen to the restatement to determine whether the listener has heard and understood the assignment to that point. It is also important that the delegator listen carefully to the restatement to make himself clearer about the task, its background, context, audience, purpose, and parameters.

Rule 3: Reflect

The delegatee should also be directed to include an occasional reflection with the restatement. Reflection is the listener's guess at the emotional component of what the delegator is asking: "I'm hearing that you are anxious about this part of the project." A purpose of reflection is to test not only one's intellectual understanding of the communication but also the larger human context in which the communication is made. Psychologists tell us that we get only 10 percent of the meaning in communication from the words used, and that 90 percent of the meaning comes from the nonverbal: tone, body language, and gestures. For example, when you come home at the end of a long day at work, your significant other asks you, "How was your day?" You reply, "Fine." Consider how "Fine" can change in meaning, depending on how quickly or slowly you say it and the inflection you use.

Reflection is difficult, for many reasons, because it is not part of the typical law-firm conversation. Nevertheless, it can be valuable, and this exercise can assist the participants in discovering its value. In this context, consider how emotional perspective can motivate and inform the listener in a variety of ways. Is this task important to the delegator's career at the firm, to his relationship with the supervisee, to his goal of doing the type of work he wants to do? Is the task tedious, but vital, intellectually challenging, and complex? Is he overwhelmed by other work, focused on this task, distracted by other things at the firm or in his personal life?

After the demonstration round is complete and the participants are working together, the facilitator should move from pair to pair, listening to ensure that the "No questions" and "Restate and Reflect" rules are followed. With gentle encouragement to stay with this format, the participants find that their conversations will take on an unusual character. Reflection is a valuable skill and an important way to build friendships and intimacy that can be crucial to a fuller teaching relationship. It can open discussion of professionalism issues as well as helping both delegator and delegatee find meaning, balance, and perspective, thereby enriching each participant's understanding of the practice.

When reflection has given a delegatee a broader understanding of how the delegator is thinking about the task, the delegatee is more likely to want to take ownership over the work and to think of ways to meet the delegator's larger goals. Conversely, being on the receiving end of reflection will also spur the delegator to dig deeper into his own understanding of the problem. In this way, reflection assists the delegator to be clearer, which will make for a more effective delegation.

Rule 4: Repeat restatement and reflection until understanding is confirmed

The participants should be told that the delegatee will continue to restate and reflect until the delegator is satisfied that he is understood. When that happens, they will switch roles.

In debriefing, the facilitator may wish to point out what the participants learn about delegation from using this format. First, the exercise points out to the delegatee the difference between listening and problem solving. It forces the delegatee to distinguish these two skills and to use them deliberately to gain understanding before she becomes "distracted" by solving the problem.

From the perspective of the delegator, this exercise also teaches that during the assignment phase, the delegator is often a work-in-progress. In fact, the delegatee can provide the delegator with a tape recorder or mirror to help the delegator see and hear where he is confused or uncertain about the goals of the assignment or even its specifics. In fact, the listening exercise can be a device for helping the senior lawyer better understand what he wants to accomplish from the assignment. It can help him discern not only what he thinks about a project, but also how he feels about it (e.g., whether he is afraid of failing, unsure about his competence, angry with the client for the client's role in creating the problem, etc.). Such feelings are often vehicles for better insight into the problem itself.[19]

In the context of giving and receiving assignments, learning to listen first for understanding can be further encouraged by the following variations. If the assignment process takes place in a conference room equipped with a white board, the junior lawyer can write down the assignment on the board as it is given, as a brainstorming device. Alternatively, the junior lawyer can restate at the end of the delegation her understanding of what she has been asked to do, or can reduce that understanding to writing in a follow-up e-mail.

One variation on the drill is to add a rule requiring the delegator to write down the assignment to hand to the delegatee. If clarity is the maximum virtue in delegation, a written assignment can provide the map for getting the work done right. Some delegators find it helpful to diagram the assignment while they give it and provide the assignee with a number of steps, directional arrows, pictures, or chart of the decision making and research process the associate should follow in completing the assignment.

Rule 5: Then, in the real world, ask questions

Attorneys from over twenty different law firms have performed this exercise, and in doing so have brainstormed a list of questions that senior supervisors believe their associates should be taught to ask when an assignment has been delegated to them:

Ask:

1. Where would you start if you were me?
2. What do you expect I'll find?
3. Are there any existing models? If so, are these models different from our case?
4. How long should this work take? What is the priority?
5. Who is the audience for the written work?
6. What are the major "what ifs"?
7. What do I need to know about the client, judge, and/or opponent?

1. Where would you start if you were me?

This question can often spark more information that will efficiently lead the delegatee to the resolution of the task. Drawing on the delegator's experience, the delegatee can decide whether to start her work with a review of an existing memorandum or template, a treatise, a law review article, a conversation with someone else who has expertise, or an interview of the supervisee's employee for a better understanding of the facts.

2. What do you expect I'll find?

This question often helps the delegator to be clearer about his intuitions for problem solving. Some lawyers prefer not to answer this question because they believe that to do so will bias the research. Others feel that the information will help the delegatee decide whether to check back if the answer is not what is expected.

3. Are there any existing models? If so, are these models different from our case?

The delegatee should be sure she understands the limitations of using work from other cases or transactions as a starting point for her work on this project.

4. How long should this work take? What is the priority?

These questions help the delegatee determine whether the deadline conflicts with other work, and whether she will need help (e.g., intervention by another partner) to get the work done on time. It also helps the delegator think about the length of time the project should take, whether the value to the client will be worth the cost, and whether the completion of this project might delay other work that needs to be done.

5. Who is the audience for the written work?

This question can help the delegator to be clearer about what is expected. If the memorandum is meant to be a quick answer for the delegator's eyes only, it needs less care than if it is intended to be copied into a letter to the client or written as a brief for the court.

6. What are the major "what ifs"?

This question helps the delegatee to develop the professional judgment which is at the heart of efficient and high-quality supervising. From the answer, the delegatee will learn in what ways the delegator has thought ahead (or not) about what may develop next concerning this project. If the task starts to look troublesome or like it will be very expensive to complete, how soon should I check back with you? If the answer seems to be the opposite of what our client wants, how creative do you want me to be in framing the support for the result we want? How far should I go for my analogies? How comprehensive the search? How detailed the case?

7. What do I need to know about this client, judge, and/or opponent?

This question can be a bridge into a deeper teacher/learner relationship because it will open up a conversation about the broader context for the assignment. It will remind the supervisor to explain whether there are budget or processing constraints put on the work by the client. It will help the delegator remember to describe the preferences of the judge or past experience with the judge that may inform how the work should be handled. Finally, it opens up the conversation to the dynamics of personality and the role that the opponent's personality and behavior can play in the approach the junior lawyer might take.

Putting these two steps together, for example, a lawyer might give the following assignment. Remember that the use of charts, lists, and diagrams can really help make the assignment clearer:

> Terry, would you come down to my office a minute? I want to bring you in on a deal I'm working on.
>
> Thanks for coming down. I know from Pat that you are between projects and that the classic M & A work is down. I thought you might be interested in working on an energy deal. It is the sale of 1) capacity, 2) an energy firm, and 3) ancillary services to enable the buyer to resell energy in a secondary market. It will give you great experience in putting one of these deals together and special expertise in helping understand how federal and state regulations can affect a deal like this. It is also a great way to look at pricing commodities where there is a long-term need and a likelihood of major price fluctuations over the life of the deal.
>
> I know you will have a lot of questions, so let me talk a little upfront to give you the context for the deal. We represent the seller, Enronic. It is a long-time client and a leader in the energy business. The buyer is the State of California. The deal is set to close in thirty days. You and I will be putting this together.
>
> First, to give you some context, let me explain a little about how Enronic buys and sells energy in the U.S. marketplace, and then I'll give you some direction about where to start in drafting the documents. This supposedly unregulated business is in fact heavily regulated on the federal and state levels. The good news is that Enronic already has a similar deal with California, but there are some important differences.

Let me start by showing you a chart for Enronic and its structure for providing energy services. Then I've set out a set out a side-by-side list of the major terms and the differences between the two deals.

All right, let's see where we are. What do you understand so far about the deal?

[RESTATEMENT]

Let me add some details. The differences between the deals start with the quantity of energy California wants, but more importantly, the flexibility they want in pricing. I have some ideas here, but I want your suggestions and creativity on this, too.

Check in with me. What do you understand so far about the differences in the deals?

[RESTATEMENT]

Now, when I delegate work I like to make sure I provide a clear set of directions on a number of points.

If I were you, I'd start by doing some background reading. I'd read through Enronic's description of the services it provides and this article on buying and selling energy in today's energy market. It is the best overview of the market I know. Then I'd get my hands on the previous deal and outline the differences between that deal and this one.

Would you get back to me by Friday with the outline?

Once you've outlined the structure of the new deal, you can start on the drafting. I want a final draft in two weeks so that we can go over the draft with the client. The draft should be the best work product you can do. We should talk about this more when you get your outline to me, but if you have questions for the client, check the file or ask me. If you can't find the answer and I'm unavailable, you can always call and ask Jim. He works on these deals all the time and I'd ask him before going to the client directly.

Finally, I have previously dealt with a deputy in the California attorney general's office, Riley Rhadert, on these deals, and he is a good guy. Of course, he will try to seek the maximum pricing benefit and flexibility for the State, as well he should, but we will have to fully understand any pricing model he proposes so we can advise the client accordingly.

Any questions or concerns? If any come up, do not hesitate to ask. E-mail is probably the best way to reach me.

• CHAPTER THREE •

Giving Feedback in a Learning Organization

THE PRACTICAL LIMITATIONS OF MENTORING AND PERFORMANCE EVALUATIONS

Mentoring, discussed more fully in Chapter Six, often provides an ideal vehicle for the development of expertise. However, there are many challenges to implementing effective mentoring in a law firm. Realistically, mentoring takes an enormous amount of time: listening time, teaching time, counseling time, and negotiating time. It is also hard to force a mentoring relationship on anyone, either the neophyte or the expert lawyer. Moreover, a formal mentoring program may not be well suited to facilitate development of supervising expertise, particularly in larger firms where firm structure allows limited early interaction between a junior supervisor and the senior members of the firm.

Some firms look to their evaluation and compensation process as a more realistic and consistent way to provide the junior lawyer with performance feedback. Most law firms today do a conscientious job of collecting evaluations from supervisors and synthesizing these evaluations into constructive sessions designed to give the associate an understanding of how she is performing.

Yet as a practical matter, the yearly evaluation process does not provide usable information to the associate on how to improve. Specifically, there are a number of limitations to the use of evaluations as the sole or principal way to provide the junior associate with feedback:

- The feedback is too infrequent. Most firms have formal evaluations only once a year, and even the more energetic firms commit to the process only twice a year.
- The feedback is too remote in time from the "performance." Associates can easily deny the reason for the criticism because the teaching moment is long gone.
- Evaluations tend to focus on how the associate is doing compared to others. It is often too vague to provide much in the way of specific direction.
- Evaluators often have motives to be less than candid in their written annual evaluations. For example, if a senior partner shares with her partners that a junior lawyer working with her has weaknesses and shortcomings, even though his performance is mainly strong and his potential noteworthy, that junior lawyer may suffer from her candor if other partners are not committed to being equally candid concerning the "squires."
- Junior lawyers tend to be defensive about the criticism that they receive. It takes an extra measure of self-confidence both to hear the criticism and then to do something about it. It is often easier to start looking for a different job than to use the feedback to motivate the attainment of new and better skills.

- Firms often lack follow-up efforts designed to get the associate the training they need to address the identified shortcomings.

The effectiveness of the evaluation session is enhanced if it is regarded by both the firm and the junior lawyer as an opportunity to set professional development goals. Ideally, the associate is encouraged to take ownership of her career. Some firms emphasize this aspect of the evaluation process by encouraging the junior lawyer to do a self-evaluation. Using a variation of the "management-by-objectives" methodology, an associate can set out measurable objectives for herself each year and then review her performance at year's end in light of these objectives. Such objectives might include gaining expertise in taking expert witness depositions or becoming efficient at managing due diligence on corporate acquisitions. By setting objectives, the junior lawyer can learn to think more strategically about her career development.

Junior lawyers should be encouraged to think creatively about the means to accomplish their objectives. If a developing lawyer wants to better learn how to manage a case, he may seek out opportunities to sit in on client counseling sessions with senior lawyers, or he might stretch to take on *pro bono* matters on which he would be the primary case manager. Similarly, a lawyer who wants to become a better speaker might join Toastmasters. If she wants to become a better writer, she might seek out opportunities to teach legal writing at a local law school or to edit articles for legal publications. A lawyer who wants to develop a particular substantive expertise will look for opportunities to work on specific cases, lead a firm seminar on the subject, or to work closely with someone at the firm who has that recognized specialty. A supervisor might be able to suggest activities that would help an associate advance toward her objectives. Additionally, there is an option that can be used instead of, or in addition to, time-consuming mentoring and annual evaluations: efficient real-time feedback. While evaluation systems can provide somewhat effective feedback, they cannot create the learning paradigm necessary to keep the firm on the cutting edge of an evolving service market. Instead, senior supervisors should look for teaching moments and provide brief directives and efficient feedback to create a learning environment that is most beneficial to all of the firm's associates.

WHAT FORM MIGHT THAT FEEDBACK TAKE?

When my daughter Kara was twelve years old, she undertook a rigorous dance program. One evening when she came home from dance, she was quite excited. It seemed that Mr. Mateer, her instructor, had spent some time with her. He had given her two pieces of advice: the first, something about how she was holding her hands that was very helpful, and he also explained a way of thinking about a step that really helped her complete the step successfully. But more important than the specific advice was the fact that he had spent two short moments advising her personally. She was on top of the world. "You see," Kara explained, "Mr. Mateer doesn't spend his time on you unless he believes you have a future." That year Kara soared as a dancer and as a person. I learned how effective even short, individually directed critiques are to the development of skills and confidence for life. They can be enormously helpful for providing inspiration and motivation to learn.

The same confidence-building experience can occur in a firm as a result of the junior lawyers' most offhanded and brief encounters with senior supervisors. A senior lawyer might take the time to introduce the new associate to the client: "This is Mary Jones. She is one of our brightest and most able associates. She will be handling most of the document production. I wanted to give you a chance to meet her in person." Or, "I liked your insight about how the court might be more persuaded if we resist making our argument overly simple, bordering on condescending. You are right that if things are too simple they can appear condescending, and it is good to add a policy reason, even where the language is clear."

These words of recognition sow seeds of confidence and fuel growth that can be enormously helpful. Such encouragement can provide the early success experience that athletes, musicians and experts from all disciplines describe as a common path to their success.

PRINCIPLES OF EFFICIENT PERFORMANCE FEEDBACK

A. Practicing before the Game vs. Coaching during the Game

It is important to distinguish the setting in which this feedback or teaching/learning might occur. One such setting is practice: analogous to a dance lesson, music lesson, golf lesson, or basketball practice where you leave the performance or game for a time and focus on practicing component steps or skills. During practice sessions, the learner is taught to work intentionally on certain skills and parts of skills so that when he later performs, he can perform at a higher level.

This kind of practice is important at every level of expertise. For example, every summer during Michael Jordan's professional career, he returned to North Carolina and worked on a part of his game. He would ask one of the coaches to help him work on a particular skill he wanted to improve. He was not satisfied with last year's performance and wanted to improve his game every year. He saw his job as a basketball player as a lifelong process of striving for excellence. Whether motivated by fear of the competition or a personal drive for excellence, he sought out the opportunity for intentional practice to refine his already amazing skills.

In law firms, the practicing and learning/teaching of individual skills often is accomplished by using simulations. Some law firms replicate this kind of practice for their associates and for those who supervise them. Kirkland & Ellis each year calls all of its litigation associates together for four days to try a case. Each litigation associate must stop what she is doing to learn a new set of facts and to conduct direct and cross-examinations, openings, and closings in a simulated trial before senior partners, jurors, and judges. As a result of these yearly practice sessions, each associate who is considered for partnership has had the equivalent of eight or nine jury trials. Other firms such as Jones Day conduct an integrated set of courses designed to match what associates need at each stage of their development at the firm. Accordingly, the firm sponsors courses in interviewing and fact investigation; motion practice; depositions and expert witness depositions; negotiation and mediation; and technology in the courtroom. To prepare the coaches, the firm conducts training programs in giving feedback in these practice sessions. The firm also sends its senior associates to NITA trial programs to receive critiques from senior trial lawyers from outside the firm. Many other firms have similar practice simulations for their junior lawyers and supervisors. Some do the training in-house. Others send their associates to NITA public programs on Taking and Defending Depositions, Expert Testimony, Motion Practice, E-Discovery, Advocacy in Mediation, and Advanced Negotiation and Mediation because they want their associates to learn skills from lawyers from all types of practice in a setting where they are protected from other senior lawyers who request immediate help on their projects.

In addition, one Houston law firm's appellate section has created a particularly innovative and effective training experience for both partners and associates simultaneously. The senior attorneys select an appellate case on which they are currently working, and everyone—partners and associates alike—takes turns delivering videotaped arguments and receiving critiques from state and federal appellate judges who are retired and/or sit outside the jurisdiction. Participation by the partners demonstrates to the junior lawyers that those partners are still interested in learning and also sends a strong message about their commitment to keep the firm a learning organization. The camaraderie that develops through this kind of practice session is truly remarkable.

Another kind of teaching, however, goes on while the "game" is in progress. You might think of this as the kind of coaching you might receive from a coach during the game. The focus is on winning the game—i.e., providing the client with excellent service—rather than creating a learning experience for the supervisee. Still, it is in these moments, in the heat of the game, that feedback can be delivered in short, effective teaching moments that create an environment for excellent service and learning.

For example, a deal lawyer might lean over to an associate during a negotiation and whisper: "At the next break in the conversation, would you summarize for us what each side's position is on the pricing term? Also summarize the underlying need behind each side's position. Do their side first, then ours. It will help us demonstrate we are listening to them and give us a chance to think more creatively about how to merge our positions."

Similarly, a litigator might ask to take a break during a deposition and whisper to the associate deposing the fact witness: "You have hit on a key conversation. Make sure you exhaust the witness's memory about that conversation. We do not want to be surprised at trial about what the witness remembers from the conversation. Make sure you ask what else the witness remembers until the witness's memory is exhausted. Ask, 'Is that all you remember of the conversation?'"

NITA teaches the art of critique in the setting of its

learning-by-doing programs. The same feedback model has tremendous value for use on the job. Such immediate feedback develops the habits that clinical legal educators have identified as essential to the skillful and ethical practice of law. It also models and thereby encourages a self-aware approach to practice: i.e., helping the young supervisor to examine what he has just done, with the goal of creating a learning model that will help him perform even better the next time.

Significantly, this feedback model assumes there is little time for feedback, which corresponds to the reality of law practice. Clinicians in law-school settings might recommend a more leisurely approach to providing feedback, starting each feedback session with a Socratic interview of the junior supervisor to determine how the supervisor feels she did. NITA's model, however, assumes a more direct approach, and assumes the teacher has an expertise that allows a more authoritative approach to learning. The model also requires specificity in comparing the learner's performance with the desired performance, thus allowing the learner to discern the "take-away" as something she can incorporate into her own style rather than just a pet peeve of the teacher.

B. Characteristics of Efficient Performance Feedback

To make feedback most efficient, the teacher and the learner should share a common language concerning the skills to be learned. The shared language becomes a shorthand that focuses the learner, with the fewest words possible, on the skill about which the teacher is going to give feedback. For example, if a tennis coach were allowed to give pointers during a match, noticing that the player's toss on the serve was not high enough, he might yell, "Get your toss up."

A golf coach, noticing that the player was not lining up toward the hole as they had practiced, might say, "Check your alignment." Similarly, the lawyer supervisor might notice something about a lawyer's approach to a key conversation in a deposition and say, "Make sure you exhaust and bookend the conversation." When lawyers have spent time working together, they likely will have developed a shared language that will allow for more efficient critique.

Even if lawyers have not had the opportunity to work with each other over time, there are other ways to develop a shared language for skills learning. In-house simulated practice sessions of the type we have discussed would build a base of common terminology for relevant skills. Alternatively, a supervisor might provide the supervisee with a book on the subject skill. NITA has a number of books in its Practical Guide series that are excellent for developing the shared language of skill development: Lubet, *Modern Trial Advocacy* 3d Ed.;[20] Bocchino, Hoffman & Malone, *Effective Deposition* 3d Ed.;[21] Zwier & Bocchino, *Fact Investigation;*[22] Malone & Zwier, *Effective Expert Testimony* 2d Ed.;[23] Guernsey & Zwier, *Advanced Negotiation and Mediation Theory and Practice* 2d Ed.;[24] Zwier, *Legal Strategy;*[25] and Siemer, Rothschild & Zwier, *Teaching Legal Strategy,*[26] to name a few. In the area of teaching legal writing, Armstrong and Terrell have an excellent book on helping to teach the principles of good editing.[27]

Efficient, meaningful feedback must be brief. It cannot distract from the service to the client (i.e., the playing of the game). Just like a basketball player who is so worried about disappointing the coach that he does not focus enough on the game, a supervisee who receives too much feedback while the game is on the line can become distracted. In addition, too much feedback can overwhelm the supervisee's confidence. Keep the critique brief and focused. Choose one point for your critique, or at the very most two. Limiting feedback to one or two points requires a great deal of discipline and restraint, particularly when there are a number of important learning points brought up by the supervisee's performance—and the supervisee desperately needs to learn them all. It may seem that limiting the learning to one or two points is inefficient. If all these learning points are implicated by this deposition transcript, why not teach them all at once? The answer is obvious when the focus is on the learner. If the teacher makes five points, how many will the learner retain? The answer is: certainly not five; likely not one; most probably zero. The supervisee is more likely to be thinking about revising her résumé for her next job-search than about all the pearls of feedback wisdom she has just received. However, if the teacher makes one teaching point, the learner will almost certainly retain that point. Remember that it is not necessary to teach everything at once. There will be another deposition, another brief, another feedback opportunity. If the supervisee can master on this occasion the skill of exhausting one deposition topic before moving on, then at the next deposition she can absorb and learn the teaching point that was held back the previous time.

Given the practical limitation of making one point at a time, a good supervisor must choose learning points carefully. In selecting which of several points to discuss, it is helpful to direct the feedback to the associate's current level of skill development. The supervisor should focus on what this supervisee needs most, and on what the supervisee is ready to learn. For example, a young piano player may not be ready to focus on dynamics and expression when she is developing the technical proficiency to give her the finger speed she needs to make a particular run. Similarly, a lawyer may not be ready to learn how to lead a deposition witness into overselling his case until he gets caught in a lie if she still needs instruction and experience in exhausting one topic before moving to the next.

The supervisor should focus the critique on the supervisee's performance and not make the critique a personal attack. Avoid comments like: "Here is a quarter. Go call your mother and tell her you've decided to go to dental school," or "You do not understand what it means to be a lawyer if you waive rebuttal. Do not ever do that again," or "Help me, what were trying to do with that line of questions?" These might all be techniques that were once used on you, but they are better coming from a drill sergeant than a supervisor in a law firm and are too personal to be effective at changing behavior. Critique what you see, not what happened during preparation the night before. You often will be giving the supervisee help in how to better prepare, but by critiquing only what you see, it is more likely that your critique will be helpful: For example, the supervisee's preparation might have been extensive, but his anxiety was so great that it got in the way of the presentation.

Most importantly, the value of feedback is directly proportional to its specificity. If the supervisee does not understand what aspect of her performance was deficient, she has little chance of learning how to fix it. Comments like "That was awful," or "What were you thinking?" or even "Not bad, you'll do better when you get more experience," are too general to be helpful.

Critiquer-Centered Personal Critique

- Comments are general
- Criticism: "I didn't like what you did."
- Criticism: "You were wrong."
- Results from focus on client, impatience
- Judgmental

Learner-Centered Performance-Based Critique

- Comments are specific
- Criticism: "This is how to do this better."
- Focus on: "What can I fix?"
- Requires time, effort, and teacher mindset.
- Nonjudgmental
- Critique the performance, not the student
- Brief and to the point

Obviously, yelling out a point of critique during a deposition or a negotiation, or while a junior lawyer is writing a brief, is impractical. What you are looking for is a break in the performance—right after, or in-between drafts—to find a short moment to give some feedback. With respect to oral performances such as depositions or negotiations, where the feedback will be given in person rather than in writing, look for a way to take the junior lawyer aside and in private ask if you might give her a quick suggestion. Recognize that the more public the critique, the more threatening it will be to the junior lawyer. Make sure to set the stage for giving the feedback so that it will be heard, understood, and believed. To the extent that it is true, you might start by saying, "You are doing fine. Let me give you a couple suggestions for going forward to make it even better." Acknowledge the difficulty of the supervisee's task, or empathize with her for being thrown into a situation without much instruction, and then offer your suggestions in a positive, forward-looking manner.

THE FOUR ELEMENTS OF A NITA CRITIQUE

NITA's four-part critique model was developed in the 1970s in its trial-advocacy courses and later formalized in its teacher-training program. The model is used by NITA teachers across the country to teach all manner of skills including fact investigation and interviewing; taking and defending depositions; examining experts; negotiation (deal making and in litigation) and mediation advocacy; motion practice; legal writing; combined specialty-skills courses in ethics; intellectual property; the crime-fraud exception to the attorney-client privilege; interviewing and counseling the client and negotiating with the opposition about E-discovery; legal strategy and the business client; capital murder defense; prosecuting in cases involving spousal abuse; and negotiation and mediation of family law issues. It is designed to help skilled and experienced trial lawyers, litigators, and deal makers work with junior lawyers in learning-by-doing workshops, and to give critiques that will be heard and adapted by the junior lawyer to his own style and personality. The model, which eschews personal critiques and war stories, has become the hallmark of NITA's learning-by-doing programs.

A. Preliminary Issues

As with all learning, before jumping in to give feedback, the supervisor should first think like a teacher. To ensure maximum learning occurs, the teacher should try to control the context for learning. The teacher should ask herself: Is this the right time for me to give feedback? Am I too angry or emotionally involved to be clear and helpful? Am I the right person to give the feedback or should it come from someone else? Do I have the time to involve the associate in fixing the problem, or do client demands require I fix it and then do the teaching after the deadline has passed? Am I partly to blame?

In addition, the teacher should think of where best to give the feedback. Should the associate be called to your office? Should you go to their office or meet in a conference room? What type of setting will allow you to best control the amount and type of feedback you want to give?

Is the subject matter personal? Does it deal with dress, physical appearance, manner of speech, tone, ethics, or professionalism issues? Did the supervisee miss a deadline or fail to present even a minimally competent draft? Has the supervisee received instruction previously on this issue? Is it a personal pet peeve of the supervisor? In what stage of learning development is this associate? Have I worked with this associate before and do I have the kind of relationship that will allow my tips on this subject to be effective?

Finally, what sort of icebreaker or introduction will initiate the conversation? Will I be able to begin with a genuinely specific compliment on how the supervisee is doing? Or will the introduction simply be, "Do you have a minute? I wanted to give you some feedback on how you are doing"?

B. The NITA Feedback Model

Four-stage critique:

- Headnote
- Playback
- Rationale
- Prescription

The Headnote

The first part of the critique, the Headnote, is the topic sentence of the critique: for example, "I want to talk with you about using leading questions on cross-examination." The headnote helps the supervisor to focus the feedback on a specific point, crisply identifying the most important thing he needs to say in the time allotted. The supervisor will not try to fix everything but will pick out a point of critique appropriate to the supervisee's learning stage.

The headnote also helps focus the supervisee on what he is about to hear. Remember that the supervisee almost certainly has an elevated adrenalin level at the moment the critique begins—if not from the performance itself, then from the anxiety of anticipating what the supervisor might say. Adrenalin may be helpful during the task, but it is generally not considered conducive to calm reflection. By stating clearly at the outset the subject of the feedback, the supervisor helps the supervisee focus on the substance of what follows rather than being distracted by trying to figure out, "Where is this going?"

By leading off with a headnote, a critiquer will also be better able to resist starting with an overall evaluation such as, "I'd give you an 'A' for effort," or "That was about a 'B' first draft," or "I'd say this isn't even a first draft." Such lead-ins tend to focus the supervisee on the fact that he is being evaluated and make it more difficult for him to listen to suggestions for improving performance. Implicit in this feedback method is the premise that everyone, no matter how skilled, can focus on doing something better. Whether you are Tiger Woods working on your drive or a beginner struggling to clutch the club correctly, good coaching helps the learner deconstruct what she is doing and start doing it more intentionally, thereby helping her to do it better. Examples of common headnotes with lead-in phrases include:

- "Let's talk about…"
- "Let's focus for a few minutes on … [In negotiations, the assessment phase of your negotiation or dealing with anger; In impeachment, the commitment part of your impeachment or the confrontation stage; In depositions, the form of your questions during the discovery phase, or listening, follow up, exhaustion, or bookending."]
- "You are coming along nicely…"
- "Nice first try at this. … I can see you've put a lot of effort into this. Now let's focus on your introductory paragraph and the need for a theme statement right up front."

Framing a headnote is hard work. The supervisor must know where she is going before she starts. In casual conversation, headnotes are unusual, often because we do not know exactly what the topic is when we start talking. The work of framing an appropriate headnote places the burden on the supervisor, rather than the supervisee, to figure out what the subject is.

Headnote

- Covers a Specific Behavior Topic
- Focuses the Critique
- Derives from the Playback

The Playback

The second step in the critique, the Playback, is a specific recitation of what the performer did that gave rise to the critique: "You asked on cross-examination, 'Why?'" In a NITA class, where the performance has been recorded, the playback is the literal playback from a recording of the part of the performance that needs improvement. Where no recording is being made, the supervisor must substitute words for the recording and must be able to play back specifically the point where the problem arose. This requires that the supervisor focus on the learner and take great care to recount the performance accurately.

To be credible and effective, the playback must be specific. Otherwise, it is easy for the supervisee to deny that the alleged misstep actually occurred. Compare two forms of playback for a cross-examination performance: 1) "You asked a number of open-ended questions." 2) "You asked, 'What did you see when you arrived?' 'Why did you go there?'" The former allows the supervisee to say, or at least to think: "No, I didn't say that. You weren't really listening to me. The rest of your feedback will be off-base because you are mistaken about what I actually did." The latter renders denial more difficult, and more unlikely, because specificity lends credibility and the supervisee is more likely to remember having heard those words come from her mouth.

How can a critiquer remember the specific point where the problem happened and repeat it back with any accuracy? It is hard to do unless you have prepared yourself for creating the playback. First, you need to be focused on the performance, and have a legal pad ready to take notes when something goes wrong. One time-honored technique is to divide the pad in half by drawing a line down the middle. One half is for transcribing what the performer is doing. The other half is for making notes of teaching points including potential headnotes, prescriptions, and rationales.

By taking a "transcript" of what the junior lawyer is doing during her performance, you are recording what is happening in the event that a problem arises. This is a particularly powerful tool when the setting is a simulation workshop, where learners perform parts of exercises designed to teach particular skills. In addition, the note taking is helpful when the supervisor is present during an actual deposition, trial examination, or negotiation. If the supervisor compares the live performance with what she expected the junior lawyer to do, the supervisor is ready to comment when a problem arises. In the ideal situation, the supervisor has prepared in advance as if she were going to perform, and then while the supervisor is transcribing what the supervisee is doing, there are easy points of comparison for ready critique. It is important, however, for the supervisor to be careful to look for contextual differences from the generic application of the skill and to try to understand why the junior lawyer may have done what he has. Otherwise, the point the supervisor critiques may not have been fairly derived from the actual performance. Playback is essential for "discovery" learning. It allows the performer to see and hear for himself the issue on which he needs to work. This method makes the learning less authoritative and more collaborative, as it depends in part on the supervisee seeing the problem for what it is and having the desire to learn how he can avoid that problem in the future. Of course there is nothing really new here. Many a deposing lawyer has learned how to take a better deposition from the painful experience of having to read aloud at trial from a transcript of a deposition he took. There is no better lesson for speaking cleanly and posing crisp questions in a deposition than reading aloud to a jury your own false starts and long incomprehensible questions. Similarly, nothing teaches the importance of exhausting a topic in a deposition like having a witness in a courtroom embellish her deposition testimony with no fear of being reined in by a contradictory answer. Nevertheless, learning of the same nature can take place earlier and when the stakes are lower if the supervisor can provide specific playback and thereby give the supervisee the opportunity to "hear" her own mistakes.

The discipline of providing specific feedback keeps the critiquer focused on the learner and reduces the urge to tell war stories. Although the impulse to tell a war story may help the supervisor identify useful topics for feedback by recalling what happened to him when "he was just a lad," the supervisee will learn more from focusing specifically on the performance she just gave.

Playback

- Discovery Learning
- Demonstrates Listening
- Is Specific

The Rationale

The third step in the NITA critique, the Rationale, is the "why" of the critique. It is particularly important for learners in the both the unconscious incompetence and conscious incompetence stages (see Chapter One), who are ready to understand on a more sophisticated level the different theories and approaches that can generate a good result for the client and the case. For them, the rationale may be the most important part of any critique. It will help them make the point you are teaching portable: something they can adopt for their own and use in different ways depending on the context. For example, a beginning lawyer may lead on direct examination and think he is doing well because he is doing all the talking. He may not understand that the jury is more concerned about the witness's credibility than the lawyer's control.

For learners at any stage, the rationale makes the learning point less mysterious and less arbitrary. Many junior lawyers struggle with the notion, seemingly implicit in the environment they see around them, that there is one right way of doing things. Many supervisees may conclude that the practice approaches presented to them as ideals are driven by unpredictable and perhaps irrational pet peeves of their supervisors. However, the practice of law is not a series of tricks to be applied blindly to produce magic results. While certain best practices and firm-wide ways of doing things may be iron-clad rules, such rules are few. For example, some firms standardize the way they want associates to start depositions in certain specialty kinds of cases or the stipulations they enter into in depositions regarding how documents will be handled.

What is important for the young lawyer to realize is that the techniques she uses may vary by type of case, personality of the witness or opponent, and goals of the client. By articulating precisely why the alternative approach would be an improvement, the supervisor encourages the supervisee to make the comparison for herself and thus to internalize a commitment to the superior approach.

For example, should one never lead on direct examination at trial? While it is generally true that leading impairs the witness's credibility and detracts from her ability to tell the story, there are times when this is exactly what the lawyer should do: where the lawyer does not care about the witness's overall credibility (because, for example, the witness has a criminal record), but calls the witness only to establish a few key facts. Accordingly, a critique encouraging the supervisee to ask open-ended questions on direct examination provides a better learning vehicle when it includes a rationale that asking open-ended questions enhances the credibility of the witness.

As another example, some conventional wisdom teaches that every opening statement in a trial should start with that lawyer's side of the case. However, there may be a sound psychological reason to deviate. Negative attribution, the tendency of an audience to attribute responsibility to the first person about whom they hear, may require the plaintiff in a wrongful death case to go on the attack against the defendant first before describing the losses the survivors.[28] For example, focus groups provide evidence that if a jury hears first and foremost about the loss a mother feels when her child is hit by a car, the jury may be asking themselves: Wasn't there anything the mother could have done herself to prevent the accident? According to attribution theory, the notion that decision makers tend to hold first players responsible, the plaintiff's lawyer should start her opening with an attack on the adversary's wrongdoing. Again, the technique might vary, depending on the latest learning from social science, or with changes in evidence law, or with the composition of the audience.

The rationale for a skills technique is often multidisciplinary, found in social science, experience, firm lore, literature, and life. Identifying and explaining such rationales is what makes the practice of law a lifelong learning project. Sharing the rationale by describing how you developed your thinking and approach, who taught you and in what context, is the closest thing to telling a war story in a NITA critique. Again, while the critique should not be about you, it is important for the learner to understand the source of the advice so that he can choose how to make the technique his own. Lessons learned from watching the prominent lawyers in the firm and elsewhere are also very important sources of authority. Still, more importantly, the rationale gives the point its context, so that if the reason for the rule or technique ceases to exist, then the rule should or can be violated, or at least adapted.

Rationale

- The Why
- Makes the Point Portable
- Gives the Point Context

The Prescription

The final step in the NITA critique, the Prescription, is a description—or better yet, a demonstration—by the supervisor of what the supervisee would do if she performed the task over again. The prescription cures the problem in the playback: ***In depositions,*** by asking open-ended questions which encourage the witness to talk, or by listing the "exhaustion" questions relating to an important conversation ("Is there anything else you can remember about what was said during that conversation?" "Anything else..." until the answer is "no"!)

According to evaluations given by NITA participants, prescriptions are the most important part of the experience. These learners greatly value seeing and hearing what needs to done. The same is true in the practice setting. The supervisor needs to be aware of how she would handle a problem that arises in practice and be willing to be specific in describing what to do. For example, a supervisor might suggest that a junior lawyer use the following approach in a negotiation: "Well, it looks like we see this issue differently. Maybe the best we can do for now is to agree to disagree on that subject. Maybe we should move on and look for other areas of agreement." This suggestion can teach the junior lawyer several valuable lessons: how to deal with anger and intransigence; how to buy time; how to build momentum for agreement—all from modeling a simple statement to deal with a potential deadlock.

The prescription is often difficult to articulate spontaneously. The best NITA instructors may frame a prescription in advance: e.g., prepare a mini-demonstration of leading questions on cross-examination. Presenting a specific prescription can be intimidating because it might not work: It is a matter of putting your own credibility on the line. Still, it is almost always well worth the risk. When circumstances allow feedback in the midst of the performance (e.g., at a break in the deposition), the supervisee has a chance to apply the learning immediately and often will be able to fix the problem right away. When there is an intervening lunchtime or end-of-the-day break, or even a fifteen-minute mid-morning break, you can brainstorm with the supervisee about how she might address the problem she encountered in the next session. Sometimes, even when time is short, the best help is real-time, like a coach saying between points "move your feet" or "bend your knees" or "racket back," or during a examination, "lead!" A specific prescription empowers the supervisee to try something different next time.

Prescription

- Tell Me, I Forget
- Show Me, I Remember

IMPLEMENTING THE PRINCIPLES OF THE NITA CRITIQUE

Given the principles of learning psychology that underlie the structure of the NITA critique, note what makes the following an example of what *not* to do.

> "That was not very good. You were completely disorganized. Please be better prepared next time. But don't worry; you'll get better with experience. When I was just starting, one time I faced a similar situation. I was deposing a witness in the Texas Instruments case and I got the witness to say… and we won the case."

For the same reasons a supervisor should not emulate the example above, the following is an example of a good critique:

> "Jay, I want to make a suggestion for this next session of the deposition. ***[Headnote]*** I want you to focus in this next session on listening and following up on key conversations. ***[Playback]*** Remember, you asked the witness what he said in the conversation with the defendant. The defendant said it was not his fault. Then your next question was: 'Did you give your name to the police?' ***[Rationale]*** There are two reasons why you want to follow up and exhaust his memory of what he said. First, if the case goes to trial, you do not want the witness's story to improve in any way that can hurt you. It's natural not to want to hear the bad stuff so if we get a whiff that the witness might unload against our side of the case we have a tendency to skip to the next topic. But if you don't go ahead and ask the question now, you will be flying blind at trial with respect to the facts you do not know. Second, the witness might skip things that happened, either because he has been coached to give the shortest answer possible, or because the question caught him by surprise and he is having difficulty remembering.

He needs a context for remembering, or a hook into time and place and circumstance, to help him to retrieve accurately his memory of what was said. *[Prescription]* In this next session you need to ask a few questions to set the context for any key conversation, and then follow up to ensure that you have the witness's entire memory of the conversation. For example you should ask, 'Where were you when you talked to the defendant?' 'Who else was there?' 'Was anyone taking any notes?' 'How long did the conversation last?' 'What topics were covered?' 'What did you say about topic 1?' 'What did the defendant say?' 'Did you say anything else?' 'Did the defendant say anything else?' 'What else was discussed about what was said about that topic?' 'What about the next topic?' until the witness says, 'nothing.'"

TEACHING THE METHOD TO JUNIOR SUPERVISORS

Practicing the NITA critique method is essential to giving efficient and effective feedback. One way that supervisors can practice giving NITA critiques is by using NITA Supervisory Skills Teaching Vignettes.[29] You can also use NITA's *Winning at Deposition* DVDs to teach supervisors how to give feedback about deposition taking and defending. The vignettes lay out examples of a junior lawyer making mistakes in typical practice settings and are designed to be exaggerated to facilitate learning the critique method. First, ask the supervisors-in-training to read about the NITA critique method in advance of the teaching session. Then, schedule the training session using the *Winning at Deposition* DVDs, which might be held during a lunch hour. Divide the trainees into groups of three. One will be playing the role of the junior lawyer who delivered the performance on the DVD. The second member of the group will be assigned to deliver the critique to the performer, using the NITA critique method. The third member of the group is assigned to identify and state for the entire group the four parts of the critique that he heard his colleague deliver. Then all the other groups of three, while awaiting their turns, should prepare to give the critique as if it were their turn.

Before viewing the vignette, each trainee should prepare to take notes for her critique by dividing a legal pad down the middle of the page. While listening to the performance, each trainee should select just one or two topics to critique. After the trainees view the vignette, the second member of the group is asked to deliver her critique. Then ask the third member to identify for the group, if he is able, the four elements of the critique he just heard. If the critiquer did a good job, this task should be easy. If the critiquer did not have a clear headnote or a crisp prescription, she may start to realize the problem when she sees that her colleague has difficulty identifying the four elements in her critique. Then, ask the trainee taking the role of the performer what he will do differently based on the critique. Again, if the critiquer did a good job, this should be easy. However, if there were multiple points made in the critique, or the playback was too general, the performer will likely have difficulty articulating what he will do differently next time.

Then the facilitator will give feedback to the critiquer on her critique. The facilitator should follow the NITA format when critiquing the critiquer, thereby modeling what is being taught. For example, the facilitator should lead off with a crisp headnote (e.g., "I want to focus on the importance of limiting your critique to just one point."), followed by a specific playback, prescription, and rationale. This means the facilitator is herself taking divided-page notes to be able to give playback when critiquing the critique. Ideally, the session will be long enough so that each trainee has a chance to act in each role.

Using NITA Teaching Supervisory Skills Vignettes

- Vignette 1 is a due diligence interview in anticipation of the sale of a business. The interviewee is the company's environmental compliance officer. Possible headnotes include: beginning the interview with a statement of purpose; listening, follow-up, and exhaustion; attending to body language and defensiveness; note-taking; and dealing with nervousness. For the more adventurous, the group can discuss critiques concerning individual mannerisms (hands up over the mouth, nervous comments, repeating "Let's see"). Such critiques can lead to discussion of the appropriateness of critiquing dress and issues of personal appearance such as hairstyle or weight. Such discussion would raise issues concerning what subjects are appropriate for critique, and whether a supervisor should raise any issue or find someone closer to the supervisee to discuss more personal issues.

- Vignette 2 is a negotiation over the sale of a business. It raises the important topic of dealing with anger. In this vignette, the junior lawyer loses her temper over what she considers to be the other side's misrepresentation to her during an earlier stage in the negotiation. Other possible headnotes include: blocking techniques; listening and follow-up; making and requesting concessions; problem solving v. position bargaining.
- Vignette 3 is a deposition. Possible headnotes include: starting the deposition; listening, follow-up, and exhaustion of a key conversation; and a failure to apply a consistent organizational scheme to keep from missing key information.

Another way to put the NITA critique into practice is to ask a supervisor-in-training to think of the last time he or she felt frustrated with the performance of a supervisee. Now, think of one part of the junior lawyer's performance that the supervisor can fix and write out a headnote, a playback, a rationale, and a prescription. Take care to write a precise headnote, and check to see if it fairly gives a name to what gave rise to your feeling that something is wrong. Next, identify playback that specifically captures the frustrating moment. Then check to see that your prescription, or fix, is forward-oriented and focused on a process for correcting for the mistake. Finally, edit your rationale to ensure that it is more than "because

I said so, and I'm your supervisor," and that it describes in context *why* this change in performance is needed going forward. Then you can decide whether to deliver the critique, or whether the learning moment has passed.

SPECIAL ISSUES RELATING TO FEEDBACK ON WRITTEN WORK

There are a number of "special considerations" when discussing the subject of teaching writing in a law-firm environment. First, criticism of writing is especially problematic because it cuts to the quick of the lawyer's ego. All but the most self-confident secretly fear that they are not good writers and that it is only a matter of time before the firm finds out. The junior lawyer knows how hard it is to write well and how much time it takes, and he worries that he takes too much time to complete his best work. He may believe that he is not naturally a good writer. When he gets back his first set of comments from a firm partner, he can become demoralized and think "They found me out! Now everyone knows I'm not a good writer." In contrast to the insecure majority, he may be in the overconfident minority. He may be an unconscious incompetent who believes, despite the edit, that because he was a law review editor that he is a good writer, and naturally so. He may become defensive and attempt to avoid doing work for that supervisor again.

Second, because of the time pressures of practice, feedback on writing is typically delivered under less than ideal circumstances. The supervisor is focused on completion of the written product and the need for excellence in client service, and feedback tends to take a "less than gentle" form. It is not unusual for the supervisee's draft to have large portions crossed out with comments in the margin reading "No" or "Rewrite" or "This doesn't do it!"[30] Because teaching writing takes substantial time and effort, supervisors dealing with the pressures of practice often give no feedback at all or make comments that are less than constructive. As a result, no learning takes place and the junior lawyer makes the same mistakes again for want of feedback.

There is also a phenomenon described by many firms of a cycle of demoralization that can occur in the first written assignments given to a junior lawyer. Typically, the supervisor is frenzied and needs help on a complex project. She does not have the time to explain the project fully, and in the midst of the delegation process she sees the panic in the junior lawyer's eyes. In response, the supervisor decides she cannot really delegate the assignment to this junior lawyer but must get help from a more experienced team member. However, not wanting to convey her lack of confidence in the junior lawyer, the supervisor goes ahead and gives an assignment but does not take the time to provide the necessary context and other information. Predictably, lacking the information to do the project well, the junior lawyer fails. The supervisor cannot afford another failure and avoids giving that associate further assignments. Meanwhile, the junior lawyer knows he has failed and avoids doing more work for that supervisor. Alternatively, some supervisors, when faced with that look of panic in the junior lawyer's eyes, will decide instead to micromanage the project. The junior lawyer senses the supervisor's lack of confidence in his work, and the resulting self-doubt leads to a poor performance by the junior lawyer.

These special considerations often lead firms to fall back on their survival-of-the-fittest mentality. Supervisors give little specific feedback, and simply will not ask an associate to work for them again if they have had a bad experience in the past. Feedback on writing often resembles a version of the following: "NO NO NO!", or the dreaded double-underlined "NO." One supervisor equipped himself with a rubber stamp with which he would stamp on associates' work: "This Sucks."

Is there a better way? Firms have taken different approaches to teaching writing. A Chicago firm uses simulations designed to teach good editing skills. Over a two-day period, the firm conducts lectures on the principles of good persuasive writing. These lawyers also engage in joint critique sessions, where groups of young lawyers work with a facilitator and edit together a brief containing typical mistakes. Then they hold an extensive simulation in which junior lawyers write a draft of the various parts of a brief and then meet individually with senior lawyers to be critiqued. Other firms engage outside organizations to conduct similarly designed writing programs.

Another approach to persuasive writing is to combine editing principles with the NITA critique model. This learning-by-doing depends on a supervisor's efficient feedback. This feedback should use a shared language with an eye specific to the junior lawyer. For example, a supervisor might add a comment to a brief that says:

> The structure is good. Tinkering should be kept to a minimum. The relationship between the first and second argument needs to be clearer. The judge might think that because legislation is not required, the court can make an exception. In fact, even though legislation is not *required*, the court should create an exception here for policy reasons.[31]

The best book I have found on that subject is *Thinking Like a Writer: A Lawyer's Guide to Effective Writing and Editing* by Steve V. Armstrong and Timothy P. Terrell. This book lends itself very well to the NITA critique method. It allows the supervisor to teach the junior editor how to edit according to fundamental principles of good writing.[32] These principles become the shared language for efficient teaching and provide the headnotes for teaching self-editing skills. Feedback based on these principles allows the junior lawyer to reread her work and edit it herself in light of the principles. Armstrong & Terrell teaches that a good editor edits in stages: first setting out a map of her ideas, then looking at organizational issues like order and transitions, then editing paragraphs for topic sentences and clear examples, and finally editing sentences and words to ensure clarity and precision.

Briefly, the Armstrong & Terrell approach is based on the idea that good persuasive writing can be taught by analyzing persuasion as a set of principles: clarity, precision, concision, comprehensiveness, appropriate detail, juxtaposition, etc.[33] Armstrong, in his lecture presentations on the subject, uses the following examples to first teach the difference between style and clarity, and then helps show how using one principle, such as clarity, can teach good editing, which in turn leads to good writing:

> Armstrong tells the story of two friends from New York City who came to visit him when he was teaching English at the University of Alabama. Armstrong picked up his friends at the airport and decided to stop off at a local bar on the way to his home to introduce his New York friends to his Alabama friends. His New York friends, a man and a woman, were distinctive in their dress. The man dressed like Tom Wolfe (all in white: shirt, shoes, tie, belt, socks, pants), and the woman was dressed entirely in Greenwich Village Black (including jet black hair and makeup). You can imagine the reaction to these two walking into a bar in Alabama. After they had made introductions and talked a while, one of Armstrong's Alabama friends leaned over and whispered in his ear: "Your friends... They sure got style...." It was not a compliment. Style that draws attention to itself, for the sake of itself, detracts from persuasion.

Another story Armstrong tells helps convey the advocate's principle of editing for clarity.

> Armstrong tells of his visit to the top of Hurricane Ridge in Washington State. He asks: "Have you ever been to the top of a mountain ridge on a bright sunny

> day? On a high mountain, everything stands out … colors, flowers, plants, even the air.… You can see and hear for miles … things are clear! That is what you are aiming for in your writing—clarity of image and definition, of word-smithing, that makes your ideas stand out, like mountain flowers." His point is that a writer needs to edit her writing so that her ideas stand out as clearly as flowers on a mountain top. His story gives the rationale for the effect the brief writer is trying to achieve: the writer's point stands out clearly as if it is being seen for the first time.

Because the well-educated junior lawyer has read many examples of good writing and grammar, these examples are ingrained already into their thinking. Once the reader puts on the hat of an editor, the editor can access these examples and rules and edit in a way that improves the writing in the light of these models. The trick is to have a clear concept of what these principles are and then to develop the writer's ability to distance himself from his writing to achieve the perspective of the editor. It is as if he is not editing his own writing but someone else's.

One key to this distancing perspective is for the writer to edit her work in waves: i.e., to edit multiple times looking for different principles each time.[34] Another key is for the writer to take the time to put down the writing and to pick it up again. Since the luxury of putting down and picking up later does not exist in real-life law practice, that process is simulated by passing the work between the junior lawyer and the supervising lawyer. This joint effort allows the supervising lawyer to teach the junior lawyer how to go back and edit the work for himself. If the supervisor sends the writing back to the junior lawyer and shows him how she edited his work with that one principle in mind, then the junior lawyer can learn to do that edit himself next time around. Ideally, the supervisor can make a couple of changes regarding a recurring writing problem and then send the draft back to the junior lawyer to make the rest of the changes for himself.

The NITA method assumes that while the supervisor is making all necessary changes for the purposes of the client's case, the supervisor must then step back from the draft and think like a teacher. The supervisor will pick a point or principle and will give the junior lawyer feedback on how she might make the edit for herself next time. It is important that the teaching/editing point be appropriate for the learning stage of the junior lawyer. Depending on the ability and confidence level of the associate, and her learning stage, the following editing principles might be teaching points for feedback:

Unconscious Incompetence

- Grammar, subject-verb agreement, pronouns

Conscious Incompetence

- Mapping that fits the purpose of the writing
- Mapping follow-through
- Comprehension v. conciseness
- Audience issues
- Understanding substantive law fine points

Conscious Competence

- Edit for persuasion: introduction, organization, transitions, detail, build multifaceted arguments (law and policy, fairness), juxtaposition, clarity, word choice, precision, big finish

Unconscious Competence

- Creativity
- Edit for super-clarity and persuasion fine points
- Edit for objective writing: introduction, issue, authority, comprehensiveness, balance, precision, clarity, conclusion

Once the model has been communicated, then the NITA critique method can be very useful in developing the junior supervisor's editing skills. Once a common language is established and the learning atmosphere created, the critiquer need not teach to fix everything. (That goal might be left to the mentors.) Instead, pick one point or two, at the most, and follow the headnote/playback/rationale/prescription approach to the delivery of each point. The headnotes for editing can refer to the principles of editing discussed between senior supervisor and junior supervisor in their earlier sessions on writing. The junior lawyer can simply be asked to edit again (or next time) with that principle in mind. The senior editor can highlight a few places where the problem arises and give a rationale and a prescription. The rationale will help the junior writer understand why this is a matter of persuasion, or objectivity, rather than simply a matter of personal style. That rationale will make the point portable and will help the associate edit for himself next time.

For example, where your headnote for feedback on a brief is, "You need more authority here," the rationale should be spelled out to help the supervisee know that you are not simply asking for string citations. It is better to specify the context: "This is a not a situation in which you are citing one case for a proposition in an area of settled law. This is a situation where [the authority is counterintuitive] [there is no authority] [there is important contrary authority], so we need more and/or secondary authority to show the court that our position on the law is similar to other practice areas, or with the best and most modern thinking on the subject."

OTHER TECHNIQUES FOR TEACHING EDITING

Firms committed to teaching writing have developed techniques for encouraging the writer to take a systematic approach to editing her own work. Some firms use games or competitions; some teach a specific set of steps the writer must go through before submitting work; some set up post-deadline writing instruction; and some teach a self-assessment technique that sets individual goals and objectives for the writer and develops a system to hold the writer accountable for improving her writing.

In the game or competition model, a supervisor and a junior lawyer agree on a list of grammatical errors, "writing sins," and pet peeves such as subject-object disagreement, unjustified passive voice, or a disconnection between the body of the document and the mapping paragraph. Then each time one catches the other in an error, the guilty party pays an ante (lunch) or penalty (quarters to a jar). One benefit of this strategy is that the supervisor shows herself engaged in a lifelong learning process, open to be taught as well as to teach.

One firm's appellate group insists that every brief go through a series of edits before the document is filed. It requires that the supervisor and junior lawyer first must meet before writing begins to brainstorm the project: its facts, legal theories and themes, arriving at an understanding of the case's best facts, worst facts, best legal arguments and themes. Next, the lawyers must map out an outline and argument headings and meet with the team leader to discuss the argument organization. Then, the junior lawyer writes a draft, focusing on topic sentences and paragraph composition. Next, the brief goes through sentence and word precision edits. Finally, the introductory paragraph is drafted to capture the heart of the argument and to map the brief's structure. This firm sets up a deadline for the latter stages. The deadline allows time for the junior lawyer to do the edits himself.

For most law-firm projects, the lack of time makes such a schedule unworkable. Many firms set up a system using the Microsoft Word comment feature so that the supervisor's final edits are sent to the junior lawyer for learning purposes. Some firms even direct the junior lawyer to save her final draft and review that draft with a writing specialist after the deadline has passed.

One firm has its supervisors engage each junior lawyer in a writing self-assessment exercise every six months.

The junior lawyer is asked to assess where his own writing needs improvement and to hold himself accountable to a strategy, including self-editing, to improve on his self-assessed writing difficulties.

· CHAPTER FOUR ·

Teaching Strategy While Managing Client Work

One major reason given by associates for leaving firm practice is that they are looking to play a more creative and meaningful role in solving the client's legal issues. If that is to occur, the junior lawyer must advance more quickly into her "consciously competent" role in the firm. The firm must give her opportunities to take responsibility for case decision making. The firm must trust the associate to understand the client's goals and the objective of the litigation or the business transaction. Unless they are given such opportunities, associates will not be able to think creatively and will be confined to implementing discrete tasks without really understanding how a particular task moves the deal or case toward a satisfactory conclusion.

When the practice of law was simpler, the young lawyer was made a part of the team from the initial client interview. Thereafter he would be included to observe and to offer suggestions while the case or deal went forward. In this age of high billing rates, clients are concerned about multiple lawyers doing the same legal work and about paying the firm to do its own training. Mindful of these concerns, supervisors need to ensure that junior lawyers learn early how to manage matters but do not accomplish that learning "on the client's nickel."

Even in a large twenty-first century law firm, there are ways for junior lawyers to learn to see the big picture sooner in the matters on which they work. We discussed earlier the notion of a shared language among lawyers, working together to facilitate efficient feedback and optimal professional development. That shared language should include a model for decision making in managing cases or deals: a set of best practices for carrying out the management strategy. That shared language should be integrated into each team's work. Ideally, the junior lawyer can be taught the best practices as part of the team-building process and then trusted to perform work on her own, consistent with the best practices established by the shared language but with room for creativity.

Steven Covey, in his program tapes that accompany his book *Seven Habits of Highly Effective People,* tells a story that illustrates how "management by objective" may not always be as easy as it seems. Covey tells of trying to teach his twelve-year-old to take over maintenance of the lawn. He walked his son around the lawn and said, "Son, there are just two main things to know about caring for a lawn. You need to keep it green and clean. Green and clean! Got it?" The son said he did. One week went by and the son did nothing. Two weeks went by. Finally, after a month of his son doing nothing, Covey took his son back around the lawn and asked, "Son, what didn't you understand about 'green and clean'?" The son burst into tears and said, "Dad, I do not know how to turn on the lawn mower!"

The lessons are clear: management by objective cannot work if the delegatee is unable to perform the basic skills required by the objectives. The supervisor needs to be approachable, a resource for getting the job done. If the supervisee has no way to confirm whether he understood the goals of the project, then the delegation has failed. The supervisor must communicate the essential elements of case management and client goals. This is where a shared language for case analysis and case management can really assist the learning process.

The lawyering process, whether for a litigator or a transactional lawyer, is based in problem solving. For example, a transactional lawyer's work is largely a variation on the following problem: "How should this deal be put together to maximize client satisfaction in both the short-term and over the life of the deal?" As a litigator, the lawyer asks: "Should I settle this case? What are the chances of winning at trial?"

Of course, there are aspects of case analysis that can be done by the individual lawyer. As a lawyer gains expertise, it is often most efficient for the lawyer to simply make the decisions for the client and to fashion the advice by herself. Yet, if the expert lawyer can involve the junior lawyers in her process of problem solving, then a great deal of teaching can go on.

In both litigation and transactions, lawyers ask: "How can I best advise the client on what they ought to do in light of their goals and objectives?" Whether at trial or when a deal closes, the need to focus on client objectives becomes more intense. Some transactional attorneys argue over every clause or comma in the deal documents;

some litigators try to present every bit of evidence and "see what sticks." Unfortunately, such an approach at trial is likely to be unpersuasive, and such an approach in deal making is likely to be counterproductive. Every deal needs focus and perspective, and every case needs a legal theory, factual theory, and theme. The process of selecting the deal's pitch, or the case's theme, is where team building can best occur. This process should start when the client walks in the door.

Where your relationship with your client permits, it is always important to try to involve the junior lawyer early in the case-development process—even at the client-interview stage, if possible. This early involvement is excellent for junior lawyer morale. What better way for a young lawyer to feel good about herself than to be introduced directly to the client as: "one of our brightest young associates, who will have major responsibilities for case supervision." Involvement in the client-interviewing stage also teaches lawyer-client relationship skills. The junior lawyer can develop a better understanding of the client's needs and goals, and be able to think creatively in pursuing those goals. It can be the "green and clean" for the junior lawyer on the deal, but with the understanding that the supervisor is available as a resource to help achieve the client's goals.

By involving the junior lawyer early in case management, the supervisor can teach (and model) ways of reconciling the sometimes conflicting roles lawyers have when conducting fact investigation and doing case analysis. The first of these roles is that of a researcher, trying to discover what happened in the past or to describe accurately what is being bought or sold. The litigator tries to discover what happened: what the key players did and did not do, said and did not say, knew and did not know, intended and did not intend, and what they recorded and did not record. The transaction lawyer does due diligence and investigates the financial condition of the parties and the risks involved in the deal.

At the same time, lawyers are the producers of a persuasive story. Working on a transaction, lawyers are persuading the other party to proceed with the deal, to take certain risks, or to agree to a certain price. Litigators are selecting a story they can tell that will take into account both good and bad facts and will align with the client's demand or defense. Lawyers play the role of blocker and protector, as well as interpreter and spokesperson, on behalf of the client. They are the public relations agent or "ad man" for the client in the legal system. They are at all times the negotiator and advocate on behalf of the client.

How does the supervising lawyer reconcile herself to these two often paradoxical roles in the context of fact-investigation planning and case analysis? How can the supervisor teach the junior lawyer to navigate between these two roles? The expert has learned how to do it, almost instinctively, but if the expert can be conscious of her approach to the challenge, the junior lawyer can more easily understand the problem-solving process for himself.

Covey says about effective habits of leadership, "Begin with the end in mind."[35] To best teach the associate how to perform fact investigation, the supervisor needs to teach the associate to look ahead to the end of the process. A transactional lawyer must be taught to keep in mind what will happen if the deal goes bad. While it is true that most cases settle, expert litigators never lose sight of the fact that the client's case could end up in court.

With this mindset, young litigators are admonished to take every deposition as if the case were going to trial. Transactional lawyers are taught to be aggressive in writing provisions for the client, because this approach leaves room for the client to make concessions as the deal heads toward closing. The drafter is taught how to develop perspective to edit his work: to imagine the deal fails with regard to a key provision in the contract. How will later decision makers know what was intended by the contracting parties from the language in the contract?

For junior lawyers to understand how they can fit into the problem-solving process of the case, they need to understand the endgame requirements for the client. The lawyer must prepare to present the client's case or deal with three different theories in mind. These are the **legal theory,** the **factual theory,** and the **persuasive theory** or **theme.** A litigator who understands the interplay between these three theories in the endgame of litigation will be better equipped to investigate facts, to analyze the case, and to prepare for settlement or for final trial. In the same way, this understanding will help the deal lawyer know how to frame the elements of the deal to best protect the client and to produce the best deal for the client. Moreover, the case-analysis process can be an excellent vehicle for individual lawyers working on the case to come together as an effective, functioning team.

LEGAL THEORY

In the NITA book *Fact Investigation,* the authors describe the various components of case analysis.[36] It may seem obvious and even trivial to say that a lawyer needs to have a legal theory in mind when he conducts fact investigation, but many judges and juries recall trials presented when the lawyer seemed to have no idea what her legal theory was. In addition, there are many deal lawyers who will wonder whether their opponent even understood the deal. A clear and compelling legal theory can help persuade a decision maker to proceed with a deal or to decide the case in favor of the lawyer's client. A good legal theory carries with it the power of logic: the power of the syllogism. Syllogisms come from analytic philosophy. A common example of a syllogism much discussed in basic undergraduate philosophy classes is:

Major premise: All men are mortal.
Minor premise: Socrates is a man.
Conclusion: Socrates is mortal.

The conclusion is said to be logically entailed, or necessary. The minor premise is included in the major premise, and the conclusion is driven or required by the major premise.

The advocate tries to create this same sense of logic, the logic of entailment, by stating a major premise and incorporating the facts as he thinks they are. For example[37]:

Major premise: The law provides that where a store clerk, acting on behalf of his employer, knowingly sells alcohol to an intoxicated individual, the store clerk is criminally responsible for the clerk's act.

Minor premise: In this case, Dan Jones, a clerk for the Cut Rate Liquor Store, sold Thunderbird wine, an intoxicating beverage, to Walter Watkins who was then intoxicated, and Jones knew Watkins was intoxicated when he sold him the wine.

Conclusion: Dan Jones is criminally responsible for his act.

Of course, as every lawyer knows, and as Aristotle pointed out thousands of years ago, there are very few situations in the real world where a conclusion is logically entailed. There may be some ambiguity in the major premise: e.g., does the law require that Jones actually knew Watkins was drunk, or is it enough that Watkins appeared drunk to any reasonable person on the premises? There may be problems with the minor premise: e.g., factually, did a sale take place? Was Watkins drunk? Would anyone in Jones's place have known from Watkins's behavior that he was drunk? But we focus here on the first issue: Legal problems are almost always subject to interpretation, which creates uncertainty. For that reason, the attempted legal syllogism more often than not fails as a matter of strict logic.

Still, the importance of syllogistic reasoning, or having a legal theory, should not be underestimated. For example, in the antitrust case of *United States v. Microsoft,* the lead litigator for Microsoft predicted that the court would eventually adopt a rule that would make irrelevant any motive Microsoft may have had to put its competitors out of business.[38] Accordingly, Microsoft's lawyers focused on the unique features of its operating system that could integrate the Internet into its functionality, and cared little for the anticompetitive motives expressed by its designers. Having thought through what they expected the law would be, the lawyers properly planned the questions for witnesses to create the appropriate syllogism. The corporate directors gave their answers unaware of the legal significance of those answers. When the court eventually agreed with the litigator's prediction, i.e., that Microsoft was free to redesign its operating system, Microsoft's case prevailed. Having a clear legal theory can therefore drive the result by making the case "easy" for the appropriate decision maker.

If one should have a legal theory before conducting fact investigation, then how does one develop the legal theory not yet knowing the facts? This conundrum can create uncertainty for junior lawyers that can lead to paralysis in the fact-investigation process. However, a supervising lawyer can suggest a number of practical steps to get the supervisee started on identifying possible legal theories and anticipating the areas of fact investigation. For example, the team leader might consult with other attorneys within the firm who have a particular expertise. In addition, the team leader might be able to point the junior lawyer to pleadings from other similar cases or documents from past deals that have been marked up by the senior lawyer and converted into other deals. Researching the elements of claims and defenses, simply by locating the relevant jury instructions, can do much to focus the team on potential legal theories.

It is important to compile and analyze legal theories before proceeding to witness interviewing. Legal theory will influence which facts the lawyer will address and the admissions she may seek from witnesses. For example, if defending a corporation, does in-house counsel want to first conduct an internal investigation? Will such an investigation be privileged? Does the corporation want the litigator to promise key employees confidentiality or job protection before conducting interviews? While these are factual issues, they involve the lawyer in doing some legal research and client counseling before heading off to do discovery. The procedural law, issues of representation and conflict of interest, and confidentiality concerns may each have to be determined before the lawyer proceeds to fact investigation.

While some lawyers start with the law and legal theory, others feel that having a substantive legal theory early in a case is much less important than having a factual theory. They believe that once they know what the facts are, they will find the law that fits those facts. Sometimes this approach can create enormous inefficiencies in discovery: Associates are charged with turning over every rock, without any guidance as to which are boulders and which are pebbles. Their supervisors are "minute wise, hour foolish," and fail to take the time to put the issues and the basic facts in context. Regardless of whether legal theory or factual theory comes first, at some point litigators must return to the law to build a logical syllogism. One very good source of major premises for syllogistic reasoning purposes can be found in likely jury instructions. For example, cases often turn on the credibility of witnesses, the weight given by the jury to expert opinions, the difference between direct and circumstantial evidence, or the burden of proof. Consulting the model jury instructions at some point in the case analysis process can alert the litigator to areas of inquiry he might otherwise miss.

At some point, every fact investigator needs to be aware of the endgame: trial. Although 90–95 percent of all civil cases settle, the client's decision whether to settle will be based in large part on her understanding of the likely outcome at trial. Accordingly, a legal theory is essential to providing the best advice to clients, whether it is because the client will need to understand the likely outcome of a trial or because there will actually be a trial.

FACTUAL THEORY

Not only must the lawyer have a legal theory; she must also have a factual theory before the client can reach a decision about how the suit will be resolved.[39] Although some cases turn on points of law, in most cases facts and proof are paramount. A factual theory allows the litigator to tell a cogent factual story that will persuade the opposition (in settlement), or the trier of fact (in trial), that her client will prevail. The deal lawyer must be able to understand the role of the deal in the marketplace and why it is fair and important that this deal will be constructed in a particular way.

If one has a factual theory too early in a case, might this blind the lawyer to contrary information? Might a lawyer's use of a factual theory suggest too strongly to the client or key witnesses that the lawyer does not really want to know the truth about what happened but only what fits his factual theory?

Although these are important concerns, at some point the lawyer will need a factual theory. Initially the lawyer's job is to find out what happened, but he needs to have a notion of what to look for. Otherwise, the lawyer's fact investigation is haphazard and inefficient. Learning theorists say it is better to start a learning project having a tentative hypothesis than to go in with a blank slate. As long as the learner is careful to keep his factual theory tentative, he will be better able to learn what really happened than if he has no preconceived notions of what to look for.

How should the lawyer initially decide on a tentative factual theory? There are a number of devices that can start the investigator on her way:

A. Timelines

Early in a lawsuit—perhaps before the client leaves the initial meeting—the lawyer should sketch out a timeline of key events. The timeline is a starting point that allows the lawyer to structure discovery. Most of us learn to think about events in chronological order. We learn by "starting" and then discovering what events followed. For example, a timeline in a typical commercial dispute might look like the one at the top of the next page.

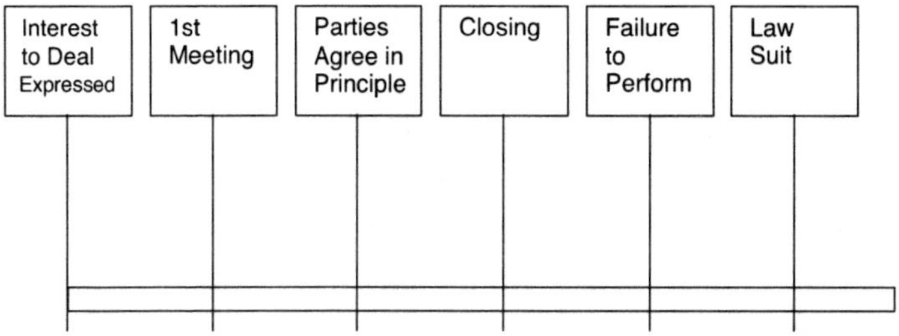

One risk of using a timeline is narrowing the focus too much to the events immediately surrounding the dispute. Putting together a timeline can help you start thinking outside the box, avoiding assumptions. Is the first event listed really the first event that is relevant to the case? Often the litigator needs to expand the timeline and ask what event(s) led up to the first listed event. For example, in a deal-gone-bad case, the timeline should start before the negotiations were even initiated, in an examination of the parties planning leading up to their expressed interest in doing business. What events led a company to deal with the other company? How did the disputing parties learn of each other in the first place? Why was the seller interested in doing business with buyer? What events led up to the signing of a contract? Was the contract a standard form with boilerplate language, or was the disputed clause specially negotiated? Who contacted whom and why was the contact made?

Reviewing the timeline will generate questions that discovery can be used to answer. While you know that a meeting occurred, you do not know what the participants were thinking at the time. What were the **motivations** of these business people for meeting when and where they met? What communications, thoughts, ideas, feelings, and emotions led up to those meetings?

In addition, the timeline generates another set of questions. What **policies or procedures** govern behavior at the time of the key events? Were there any notes taken at the key meetings? Was a secretary present? Were the meetings recorded? Was a follow-up memorandum written? Do the parties keep telephone logs of their conversations? Do the individuals have standard ways of dealing with certain matters? If they do, how were they trained in those procedures?

A conscientiously prepared and carefully studied timeline will reveal the things people did **not** do: calls they did not make, or precautions they did not take. Moving down the timeline, the litigator must start to look for key **nonevents.** These nonevents can be helpful in establishing negligence, especially where there are policies and procedures in place supposedly to ensure that the event happens, which did not happen in this case. For example, if an executive committee is supposed to review all prospective purchases before the deals are approved, then an absence of a record of action by this committee may raise questions as to how the deal was done.

Timelines are useful not because they answer questions, but because they raise questions. Timelines are great for discovery planning because they force the litigator to look hard at the gaps between the key events in a known timeline. A timeline can spur a lawyer's curiosity to discover the whys and wherefores of the client's story, which in turn can lead to all kinds of useful information.

B. Story Outlines

Imagine that you are about to be called upon to tell an interesting story. The process of preparing a story outline is another discovery planning device that can help fact investigators become more creative about what they might be looking for.

Ask yourself, for example: what would I love to be able to say about the opposing party if I were free to make it up? Imagining the darker side of a story can spur the imagination of fact investigators to look for those facts. This process may generate such questions as: I wonder if the other side's key witness ever got into any trouble? I wonder if they ever got caught lying, cheating, or stealing? I wonder if they are biased in any way? I wonder whom they know and whether they are at all beholden to the people they know? What skeletons are in their closets?

By the same token, a lawyer should be creative and imaginative in searching for the positive aspects of her own witnesses. What appealing things have they done with their lives? What social causes have they furthered, and what people have they helped? The lawyer's job includes accentuating the good side of her witnesses and emphasizing the bad side of the adversary's witnesses. This process is greatly aided by thinking creatively about witnesses.

Experienced lawyers recommend that the litigator write, in two or three paragraphs, the overall story he might tell, and do the same for each prospective witness. These story outlines might lead the litigator to questions about motivations, policies and procedures, and non-events, to pursue further in discovery.

C. Imagining What Really Happened

Another fact-investigation planning device that many lawyers find particularly useful is to use one's own life experiences to sort through the factual discrepancies of the case: "What do *I* think really happened in the case?"

For example, in a commercial dispute the lawyer for the seller might ask himself: Do I really think the buyer's agent is lying when he says he called the seller's secretary and asked for a specific modification to the contract? Or do I think it's more likely that he just forgot to specify what he wanted because he was in a hurry or got careless? Discovery has produced the buyer's agent's telephone log, which corroborates his request for the special provision; there is nothing to suggest that the log was fabricated or altered. This is a hard fact for the plaintiff to overcome. By asking himself what really happened, the lawyer will focus on the theory that it does not matter what the buyer's agent requested by phone, because the seller has a policy of only accepting telephone orders. Ultimately what matters is what the buyer's agent put in writing, which was a letter failing to specify insurance.

Imagining what most likely really happened helps the lawyer prepare her case in two important ways. First, it will force the lawyer to confront the **hard facts** in the case, which is far more critical to prevailing than addressing the good facts. A lawyer who does not address the bad facts in his case does not provide the jurors, who may be inclined to favor his case, the material they will need in the deliberations to persuade their colleagues. Second, thinking about what really happened will encourage the advocate to put herself in the shoes of the adversary's witnesses, to imagine what they were thinking and doing when the events in question unfolded. That empathy may cure "litigator's disease": that is, it may save the lawyer from overstating her case by ignoring obvious justifications or motives that influenced the conduct of those witnesses.

In any event, creating a cohesive, persuasive story outline can be very useful for spurring the imagination of the lawyer to look for key facts as she makes her way through the discovery process. In fact, what often happens in these story-outline exercises is that the lawyer discovers she may be able to tell more than one story about why something happened the way that it did. Then her job is to pick the most persuasive story that she can tell. Why is it important that the lawyer tell only one persuasive story? Why not tell multiple persuasive stories and let the fact finders take their pick?

Take for example the NITA problem, *Nita Liquor Commission v. Cut-Rate Liquor Store.* In this case the defendant is tempted to say that the clerk, Dan Jones, did not make a sale; but if he did make a sale, then Watkins was not drunk; but if Jones made a sale and Watkins was drunk, then Jones did not know Watkins was drunk. Trying the case on all three theories at once is problematic. The jury, hearing multiple stories, reacts like a parent hearing multiple versions of a story about what his child was doing at the time something went wrong. With each version, the hearer starts to believe that he is finally being told what really happened, and when he hears inconsistencies he concludes he cannot believe any of the versions.

Of course, in criminal cases, a defense of multiple factual theories may be all the defendant has left because the state cannot prove what happened. However, fact finders are often interested in solving the case and discovering what indeed happened. Multiple stories can create cognitive dissonance for such fact finders. If the defendant can relieve this dissonance by showing how the pieces fit consistently together, then so much the better. For plaintiffs and prosecutors, this is vital. After all, multiple factual theories expose the plaintiff or the prosecutor to the argument that they do not know what really happened, are just speculating, and therefore have failed to meet the burden of proof. The advice from most experienced trial lawyers is that if you do have multiple stories you could tell, pick the most likely one and tell it. Otherwise, the risk is high that the jury will regard the multiple theories as a smoke screen of no substance.

This advice leaves the lawyer with a significant challenge: which story should I tell? There are a few rules of thumb that many lawyers have found helpful in sorting through this problem. First, preview your stories with listeners who you know to have good common sense. What you are looking for here is someone, not in your law office or particularly beholden to you, who will candidly warn you away from the incredible, histrionic, or overly clever explanation for what happened. The not-someone-in-your-office rule may apply only to lawyers; many trial lawyers say that their secretaries serve this function splendidly. In any event, avoid relying too much on what junior associates, or even other experienced trial lawyers, may think about your clever explanations. Law office "group think" can often encourage the lawyer to take the high-risk approach of an overly aggressive factual theory that unnecessarily attacks the adversary. Instead it is better to ask: Can I sell this theory to Mom or to a good friend with common sense? It is not necessary to be able to sell your theory to a skeptic. You can control the atmosphere in the courtroom, or in a negotiation, so that the listener will find you sincere and likeable and want to believe you. Yet your theory must pass the "red face test." Can you tell it without a red face? Can you persuade someone who is standing in the real world? Knowing that you will have one factual theory rather than multiple versions of what happened will cause you to work harder to find other facts consistent with your theory. Another question a lawyer should always seek to answer is: If what I say is true, then what else would be true?

Consider again the typical commercial dispute. If you represented the seller, you might be convinced that the buyer forgot to ask for his special modification to the standard contract in his letter and that his language in his order letter was simply standard language he often used, not intended to have the particular meaning he is now trying to give to it after the fact. Your factual theory is that buyer's agent did not intend that its special modification be referenced with the words, "Please handle as per the usual agreement." If that were true, then what else would be true? It is likely that there would be other letters in his file where he uses the same standard language. It would also follow that in some of those transactions the special modification was not provided. Such a theory would at least be worth some discovery. By asking "What else would be true?" the lawyer will come to a series of questions he might not otherwise think to ask.

A related factual-theory selection criterion is to ensure that the story you tell is consistent with all the hard facts. For example, one brainstorming session with a group of lawyers about the Cut-Rate Liquor case produced the following discussion. One lawyer felt the state could not prove that Watkins bought his unopened bottle of Thunderbird wine from Cut-Rate because no receipt was found. Then another lawyer asked, "If Watkins already had a bottle of wine when he went in, why did he go into the store? Was he just doing some comparison shopping?" The question was an example of facing a hard fact. If the lawyer cannot explain what Watkins was doing in the store if not buying wine, the unopened bottle of Thunderbird wine—receipt or no receipt—is a hard fact. Perhaps this means that the lawyer must go back to Watkins and ask him whether he was stocking up for the night and then found he did not have enough money. But without some way to answer this question, it is probably better to try the case based on the theory that Jones did not know that Watkins was drunk than to argue that no purchase took place in the store. The Jones-did-not-know theory is consistent with the hard facts: that Watkins had an unopened bottle of Thunderbird wine, and that he failed the field sobriety test. Yet that theory does not concede criminal responsibility because it does not admit that Jones knew Watkins was intoxicated.

BRAINSTORMING

Brainstorming is another exercise that helps in generating a plan for investigation and discovery and a story line for negotiation or trial. This time-honored technique is used by creative problem solvers in many disciplines: business, science, government, and law. It is based on the notion that a major obstacle to creative problem solving arises when one focuses too narrowly on a story or fact and overlooks the possibilities presented by connecting facts to other major facts.

What is the risk of narrowing one's focus too quickly? Assume that you have been asked to solve the following problem: Connect the nine dots below using just four straight lines without your pen ever leaving the page.

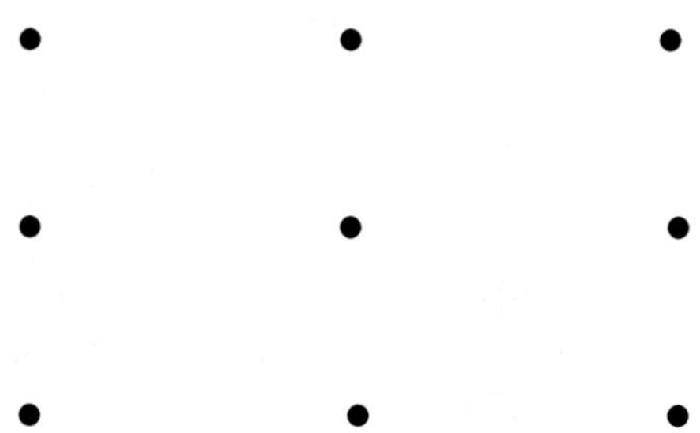

The problem is unsolvable if the problem solver sees the dots themselves as a boundary of operation. Now turn the page and consider one solution. Note that the

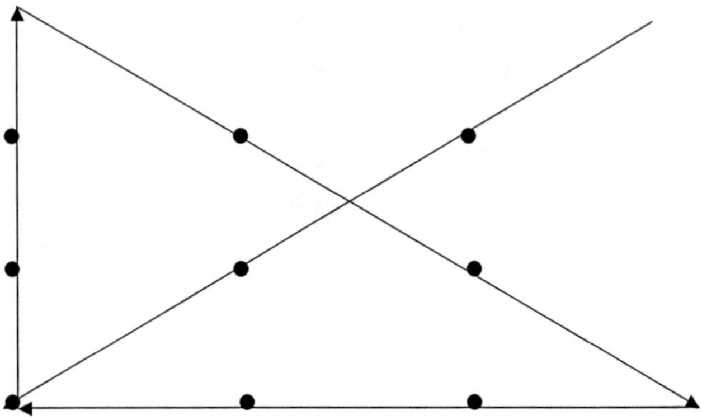

key is to extend the lines out beyond the boundary created by the dots.

Other professions also struggle with a decision maker's tendency to narrow too quickly. Our medical and business colleagues have the same difficulties with misdiagnosis. This tendency to narrow too early may come from a lack of planning time, or impatient reluctance to wade through all the facts. It might come about because the decision maker must deal with a style of learning with which she is uncomfortable: In Myers-Briggs terminology, she may be a "judger" and have a low tolerance for the process of joint open-thinking. In any event, there are obviously some real risks in recommending factual theories without engaging in comprehensive thinking. Brainstorming is one means of keeping the focus broader for a longer period and of combating learning preferences that make it difficult to think more expansively.

A system of brainstorming that has proven very useful to trial lawyers has four parts: listing good and bad facts;

listing best and worst facts; spin control; and selection of a theme.[40]

A. Good Facts/Bad Facts

Set up in a room with a blackboard, whiteboard, or easel pad. Designate a recorder. Then encourage members of the group to call out facts that in their minds are helpful to the case. No one is allowed to edit the ideas: If a fact nominated as a good fact seems like a bad fact to someone else, it still gets noted as a good fact. Debate and ranking will come later. For now, just get all the good facts out on the board.

One useful addition to this process is for the recorder to reflect back the idea to the person who proposed the idea. This has two purposes. First, it is important that the recorder writes the nominated fact and not his or her interpretation of the fact. Second, the recorder should make sure he is recording facts and not inferences from those facts. For example, it would be incorrect at this stage to record as fact that Chris Kay, in the BMI case, is ambitious. Instead, the group should call out facts that support the inference that he may be ambitious—that he was not in the office, that he was being evaluated by headquarters for a promotion, that the promotion would have meant a pay raise of $14,000–34,000, etc.

By being sensitive to the fact/inference distinction, the recorder's reflection requires that the brainstormer be precise with her facts. The recorder thus ensures that wishful thinking does not take over the process. Many group planning sessions can be affected by a kind of "group think" phenomenon in which someone mentions what may be a fact and the group latches onto it and proceeds to plan as if that fact were proven. In a recent auto-products liability case, the defense latched onto the "fact" that the plaintiff would have died anyway even if the gas tank had not exploded because he was dead at impact. However, no one had bothered to interview one of the eye witnesses who saw the plaintiff steering the pickup over to the side of the road after impact. Obviously, the defense factual theory could not withstand that one additional fact.

When the group has identified the good facts, they should then call out the bad facts. Often the group recognizes that some facts are both good and bad, depending on the spin one puts on them. For example, in a commercial dispute a buyer's two years in the business can be good if it makes the buyer the David against the Goliath, a seller who is the size of IBM or Microsoft. It can be bad if it implies inexperience and incompetence. Often recorders divide the board in half and record bad facts simultaneously with good facts.

This process of calling out good and bad facts can take some time. If the history of the case is lengthy and somewhat complicated, the recorder might break the brainstorming process into segments according to a timeline. This can be particularly helpful for getting the brainstormers to reflect more broadly on issues they might otherwise miss relating to the early history of parties, damages, or subsequent remedial measures. The recorder should encourage everyone in the room to participate. It is often in the waning moments that someone thinks of something "new" or tries out an idea that may give everyone a new perspective. Give time for the individuals to exhaust their ideas.

As the recorder looks back at the board, she should encourage the group to look for connections. Are there facts that should be grouped together? Are there connections that participants had not seen before?

B. Best Facts/Worst Facts

The group should now start to prioritize and to focus on what is most important. Each brainstormer should select the three facts he finds most important. The recorder can request that each participant write down her selection and prepare to defend her choices. Then go around the room and have participants vote and briefly explain their vote. See if there is any consensus. Where there are differences, see whether through persuasion and discussion the participants can come to agree on the most important facts. Point out that these decisions will be very important for focusing their presentations of facts.

The same process should be employed with regard to the worst facts. This is important again so that the litigators do not prematurely disregard important bad facts that strongly counter their client's position. Next, the discussion should turn to the rules of evidence and motions *in limine*. Is there any way to keep out the bad facts? Is there a way to narrow the focus of the dispute so that the bad facts become irrelevant?

Alternatively, is there now a need for more discovery? What additional facts may mitigate or overcome the otherwise bad facts? In other words, the "worst facts" brainstorming should involve a process very much like political spin control.

C. Spin Control

Advocates should consider a number of spin-control options. One is to simply admit the bad fact. Perhaps a word of explanation is in order here. In the movie *Clear and Present Danger,* starring Harrison Ford as Jack Ryan, advisor to the president and all around good guy, the president calls his advisors to counsel him on what to tell the press regarding his connection to a man who was recently found murdered off the Florida coast in a boat filled with cocaine. Ryan comes late to the meeting, but just in time to hear an aide advise the president that he should deny that he even knows the man. We also see others advising the president to say as little as possible. Ryan speaks up and advises that the president simply admit he was a very good friend of the man and feels terribly that he has died. As the rationale for his advice, Ryan suggests, in essence: "If you simply admit, then what is there to investigate? The matter will end there."

Similarly, where a witness or party, without excuse or apology, simply admits the bad fact and owns up to it, good things happen. The witness looks refreshingly honest. The audience is no longer curious about the matter and may leave it alone. If, on the other hand, the witness denies the fact, and it is later proven anyway, the matter has been made twice as bad. For example, where a babysitter is accused of shaking a baby to death, a denial that the babysitter ever shook the baby will likely affect the jury's willingness to consider the second defense that the babysitter did not intend for the baby to die.

Another way to deal with a bad fact is to justify or excuse it in some way. It is important, though, not to be too defensive. The principles of primacy and recency (i.e., people remember best what they hear first and second best what they hear last and remember less well what they hear in between) provide a vehicle for explaining a bad fact in a less defensive way. Juxtapose a bad fact with the best excuse, followed by a number of countervailing good facts, and place the whole topic about two-thirds of the way through your argument.

Alternatively, you could deny the bad fact and juxtapose multiple facts and reasons why the bad fact could not have occurred. You compare witnesses for bias, documents for contradictions and omissions, and expert testimony for inconsistencies and overreaching. Again, if the client's case comes out weak, you can also make sure to use juxtaposition with stronger arguments to de-emphasize the weakness.

THEME

A theme may be the most important way to address the things that will really matter to the decision maker. What is a theme? How does a lawyer find or create one?

Ever since the days of Aristotle, persuaders have known that audiences make up their minds not only with reason and logic but also using intuition and emotion. Aristotle described persuasion as the taking of a person to a place in the mind where they felt "at home." Aristotle called this aspect of decision making reliance on *enthymemes.* He described them as nonrational bases of decision making based on deeply held feelings or on basic norms of fairness. The world is too complex, and the need for decision making too great, for audiences to wait for "scientific proof" before they decide what to do. Persuaders have long known this. That is why they create themes for their speeches and try to persuade with attention to feelings and the heart, as well as the head.

A famous recent trial exemplifies this point. In the O. J. Simpson murder case, the defense's theme was rush-to-judgment: that the police mishandled and planted evidence to reach a foregone conclusion. The power of this theme was that it captured the underlying unfairness of the prosecution's case, made the defendant's points memorable, and pulled together the multiple parts of the defense's legal theory with a catchy idea that gave the jury comfort that they were deciding the case fairly.

This example demonstrates the importance of having a good theme that catches the attention of the jury, gives the client's case a feeling of unity, and speaks to the underlying fairness of the client's case. The power of a well chosen theme is all around us: advertisers who make us remember their products when we go shopping, politicians who repeat their campaign slogans *ad nauseam,* preachers' sermons, or titles listed on billboards. The world is filled with persuaders who have thought about the power of a carefully chosen pitch or theme.

Deciding to have a theme is only part of the job. A lawyer must find the theme that fits her case. Again, brainstorming techniques can be utilized. Participants call out a catchy phrase, song title, biblical saying, or alliteration. Another device many trial lawyers find useful in generating a theme is to write a succinct answer to the question: "Why is it fundamentally *fair* that we win?" Forget the law for a minute. "Why is it *fair* or *just* that we prevail?" The trick is: The answer must fit on a bumper sticker.

Often what happens in the "theme" session is that the group refocuses on the best facts or worst facts. Having a theme is sometimes as simple as noting an essential quote from a witness or a document. In our commercial case, for example, it could be the use of the simple phrase from the order letter: the transaction will be handled *"as per the usual agreement."* That could be buyer's theme, because it sums up their position. Buyer asked Seller to insure the goods in September (the only other transaction with Buyer) and then asked—in the same words—in January to "do it like you did in September." It's as simple as that!

Experienced lawyers say that after a while the cases they try play out on a number of recurring themes. They play out on issues of credibility of the witnesses, or the difference between direct and circumstantial evidence. They play out on the fairness or unfairness of holding someone to the burden of proof despite the fact that someone has been injured. Another recurring theme for defendants in commercial litigation is that the plaintiff is playing some version of the blame game, not taking responsibility for the choices he has made. Looking back through the history of the dispute and noting the choices the plaintiff made that contributed to his own injury can help the defense tie its case together under one unifying theme.

To a great extent, the transactional lawyer has a similar three-step approach in her analysis of any deal. The first step is to understand the legal regulatory scheme that applies to or sets the rules for the deal. In other words, the deal has a legal theory that applies to it.

For example, if a deal lawyer wants to set up a "collar option" to help General Motors buy copper from Bolivia over a number of years, she must first decide whether buying huge amounts of copper constitutes buying and selling a commodity and therefore is subject to the Commodity Futures Exchange rules. Absent an exception to that regulation, the buying and selling of options is subject to the Commodities Future Board of Exchange.

On the other hand, the client, General Motors, may have a factual story to tell and a theme for its position that this transaction is subject to an exception for large purchases of commodities. The factual theory is that where the option is a pricing mechanism that is not meant to be bought and sold on the commodities market but meant to be held by General Motors and exercised only as a part of its contract between GM and Bolivia, the reasons for the board's regulations do not exist. The factual theory upon which its position is based is that if General Motors is forced to buy and sell copper on the commodities market, it is subject to too great a risk in price fluctuations and the market is thereby harmed because General Motors is unable to insure long-term supplies of copper necessary to meets it needs. The theme is that the board's market regulations for buying and selling commodities options actually increase the volatility of the market and harm the ability of a buyer to plan in the long term what its costs of production will be. The consumer bears the costs of this volatility in the price he must pay for the automobile.

The deal lawyer may see no clear exception to the board's regulations of its options contract, but may still go forward on the deal based on the client's factual theory and the themes behind its position: that the deal is good in and for the marketplace. By understanding not only the regulations but also the role of the deal in the marketplace, the deal lawyer truly understands the deal. Understanding brings control: both control of drafting and control of the legal and financial risks for the client.

CONCLUSION

Where a supervisor can deconstruct for the junior lawyer how a managing lawyer thinks about a case—its legal theory, its factual theory, and its theme, all with the endgame in mind—then the junior lawyer can become a more creative member of the team and can more effectively assist in solving the client's problem and serving the client's goals. The same goes for taking the junior lawyer through the reasons for and strategy of putting a deal together. In the process, the junior lawyer's morale is improved. She can find ways to be creative. She contributes to the overall game plan and takes ownership over her work. Her work has meaning.

The benefit of this approach is that the case analysis process can greatly help your group to be molded into a highly functioning team.[41] As opposed to a dysfunctional team, a highly functioning team has trust in each member of the team, can engage in constructive conflict, and will put client service above the advancement of any one member of the team.

Through engaging in brainstorming, the team leader invites input from every member of the team, no matter how junior, and shows herself vulnerable and open to new ideas. By encouraging team members to express their insights about "good" and "bad" facts, the process gets buy-in from each member of the group. Each member has had a chance to contribute. Each has had their ideas written up on the board. The brainstorming process also helps the team members learn how to express insights without demeaning others. Remember that the process forbids initial disagreement and requires that at the most, an objecting member can ask that another member's fact also be listed in the opposite column as either a good or bad fact. This process shows members how to agree to disagree and come back to the disagreement when they have a more comprehensive understanding of the case or situation.

When the group moves to a discussion of best and worst facts, the case analysis leader can teach healthy, constructive conflict. Each team member should be encouraged to explain why he voted the way he voted and to support his position with good reasons. Such a process teaches good persuasion: effective arguments are backed by detail and facts, are multifaceted in their reasoning, and include appeals to the heart as well as the head.

As a result of the case-analysis process, individual team members can come together in their decisions about the case's legal, factual, and persuasive theories. Unified in purpose, the team members will be better able to take ownership over each member's tasks and to work creatively and efficiently to meet the client's goals. Just as with any sports team, if everyone is working together and understands the case theory and theme, the team's efforts will be greater than the sum of its parts.

A junior lawyer presented with the opportunity to understand the client's objectives, and how the effort advances those objectives, will be a more creative and effective contributor to the team and a more satisfied professional. The same principles that, in the context of case management, will enhance client service and supervisee morale can also build leadership skills in junior lawyers as well as their more senior colleagues. This is the phenomenon we address in the next section.

• SECTION II •

Beyond Supervisory Skills: Developing Law-Firm Mentors and Leaders

In Section I, we reviewed several techniques for effectively teaching supervisory skills in law firms. In Section II, we consider how those same skills can assist lawyers in providing leadership within their firms, with respect to practice issues and administrative and governance challenges facing the firm.

PORTING SUPERVISORY SKILLS TO LEADERSHIP CHALLENGES

In the technology world, *porting* refers to making software usable on a different machine or with a different operating system. The same concept applies to the supervisory skills discussed in Section I that enable law-firm supervisors to listen effectively, to draw out information efficiently, and to communicate clearly. Those same skills can be applied on another platform to provide effective leadership in law-firm contexts ranging from performance coaching, practice development, client management, and organization governance.

For example, in the delegation exercise in Chapter Two, supervisors learn the value of deferring questions when receiving information. Deferring questions and reflecting on what has been heard may feel strange or even uncomfortable to lawyers given their extensive training and experience in how to ask questions. However, supervisors learn that when they defer their own questions and instead reflect on what they hear until the speaker confirms that the reflection is indeed what she meant to impart, they have gained a much deeper understanding of the speaker's message. The potential distractions of the listener's wrong guesses, or unhelpful projections of the listener's expectations, have been minimized or eliminated in favor of clearer understanding. Suppose this same discipline of deferring questions and reflecting until understanding is confirmed was used by a law-firm leader who has been asked to mediate a conflict between two partners. The mediator might be tempted just to ask questions to determine, in the most time-efficient manner possible, what the issues are and what has led to the conflict. However, by asking questions too soon, the mediator might never hear how strongly the disagreeing partners feel about various aspects of the dispute and might mistakenly conclude that certain aspects of the dispute are more important to the disagreeing partners than they really are. If, instead, the mediator engages in active listening and reflects back what he hears until the speaker confirms that he has it right, he may get information about what aspects of the dispute matter most and which are relatively non-negotiable. This information may expedite the resolution and also help the mediator identify a resolution that is more satisfactory for one or both of the disputants. Another example of a supervisory skill exemplified by the delegation exercise is the discipline of not launching the project until the assignor is sure that the assignment is correctly understood and all the basic questions about resources and expectations have been asked and answered. This same discipline will serve a firm rainmaker well who is in the process of handing off client work or even a client relationship to a more junior lawyer. Taking the extra time to confirm that the junior lawyer understands the history of the client relationship and has a chance to ask questions about the rainmaker's expectations for her future involvement with the client may avert a painful client misunderstanding or even allow the junior lawyer to see a potential business development opportunity that might otherwise go unrecognized.

Similarly, all of the supervisory skills reflected in the NITA feedback model have substantial application in the law-firm leadership context. Take, for example, the headnote: the notion of stating clearly and succinctly at the outset of the communication what the topic is ("We are going to talk about leading questions."), or even a more fulsome statement including both the topic and the goal ("Let's talk about using only leading questions on cross-examination in order to keep control over the witness."). The discipline of framing a headnote before beginning one's comments greatly improves the clarity of communication and enhances the persuasiveness of the communication. A law-firm leader effectively running a meeting on the difficult issue of partner compensation would be well advised to employ the discipline of the headnote.

For example: "The next item we need to discuss is revising our compensation system to incentivize junior lawyers to manage the work brought in by the originating rainmaker."

Another "porting" example from the feedback method is rationale. As we discussed, rationale helps make the feedback point portable and elevates the suggested learning point from simply avoiding a pet peeve of a particular partner to something that will improve future work in a specific, valuable way. Whether the point is a suggestion or an instruction, an effective leader will take the extra moment to explain why this step is important to the overall process or goal. This extra information builds the leader's credibility and empowers and inspires the listener—whether a fellow partner or a file-room clerk—to do a better job because now she understands the big picture and the leader has shown interest in her participation. It is just one of the ways successful leaders build especially loyal teams.

These useful supervisory skills of listening hard and communicating clearly can be "ported" to give law-firm leaders greater success—and less stress—in accomplishing a broad range of responsibilities not directly related to accomplishing the client's work.

• CHAPTER FIVE •

Modeling: Teaching by Example

The leader teaches by example rather than by lecturing others on how they should behave.

—JOHN HEIDER, *The Tao of Leadership*

We laugh when we hear the old adage, "Do what I say, not what I do," because it is so obviously unconvincing. If the teacher doesn't do it, why should I?

Modeling is an aspect of teaching that can be one of the most effective learning tools. When a good teacher models, she is actually doing what she is suggesting the student do. In a NITA trial program, the trainer might even step up to the witness and demonstrate the technique she is suggesting. Another way to model effective communication techniques is to do so simultaneously with the giving of the critique. The clearest way to model effective communication skills is by example: deliver the four-part NITA critique standing, in a strong voice, with no notes and lots of eye contact. If the headnote of the critique is to keep the drama and energy up in the courtroom as you conduct the direct examination of the actuary, the lesson is more likely to stick if delivered in that manner than while seated, reading from notes, with eyes and voice directed at the legal pad rather than at the learner.

Under the NITA method of training teachers, modeling takes on the aspect of three-dimensional chess. For example, when talking about clarity, one must be clear; when teaching about specificity, one must be specific. When a teacher trainer is critiquing a critique, he is also modeling with his own critique the clarity of the headnote and the rationale and the specificity of the playback and prescription. If the point of the feedback is that the playback is not specific, the teacher trainer models specificity by saying, "You said to the student, 'You asked several leading questions on direct,' but you did not give her any examples." The teacher trainer is not modeling specificity in playback if she says only, "Your playback was too vague for the student to understand what she did wrong."

It is obvious that in a law-firm environment values such as respect for the individual, inclusiveness, patience, diligence, and integrity will only be effectively perpetuated if modeled from the top down. The possibilities for teaching every day are endless.

Take, for example, the painful issue of how to deal with a mistake. Of course it is useful to strive to avoid mistakes entirely, but it is unrealistic to think that they will never occur. Law-firm leaders can teach several lessons through modeling when mistakes occur. First, face the mistake and do something about it as soon as you discover it. Don't pretend it did not happen; don't hope it will go away by itself or that no one will notice. When the brief got filed without a table of contents or the communication intended for the client was faxed to the adversary, junior lawyers are likely to be among the first to learn of the mistake. The sooner the mistake is recognized and addressed, the better. Second, leaders can model how to handle responsibility, or "fault" or "blame," by refusing to blame a subordinate who did what he was told when the instructions were faulty. Senior lawyers can model a focus on fixing the problem instead of placing blame, and on remaining calm and focused throughout the process rather than becoming angry, yelling, or pouting.

In addition, supervisors and leaders can model how to handle the mistake with the court or the client by identifying it, explaining the significance and the fix, and by apologizing without blaming others. They can model how to deal effectively with staff—secretaries and paralegals, clerks and court reporters—by treating them with respect and patience. Leaders can demonstrate how to build loyalty and trust among the team by crediting each where credit is due and accepting blame where the leader has made a mistake. Leaders can demonstrate how to prepare for a difficult meeting with a client, witness, opponent, or court by engaging in role playing and moot practice sessions. Junior lawyers can learn not only how to prepare but how to think strategically for the interpersonal dynamic that is likely to affect the outcome of the meeting.

Finally, even though there may be pressure not to use multiple lawyers on a client matter, the leadership in the firm may decide that learning by example is the most effective strategy for learning important lawyering skills. In litigation, a junior lawyer might be asked to:

- Attend a deposition to watch a master at work
- Read the deposition transcripts, not only to summarize key facts and index key points but to learn how to depose or defend a deposition
- Edit a case-investigation plan for the management of an upcoming litigation
- Sit in on a client interview or counseling session to watch how the client relationship is developed and nurtured

In a transactional setting, a junior lawyer might be asked to:

- Review a deal with a senior lawyer, paragraph by paragraph, and describe what is involved as a matter of strategy, law, and economics with regard to each decision that has been made
- Sit in on a client interview to understand how the senior lawyer interviews the client to learn about how the client's goals and needs relate to the transaction
- Accompany the senior lawyer to a counseling and negotiation planning session to watch how deal-making strategy is developed and managed

· CHAPTER SIX ·

Mentoring

Mentoring is tremendously valuable when it comes to developing expertise and is the ideal way to teach and learn expertise. Learners need the encouragement and discipline of a coach to convince them that they can become accomplished in their skill development, but also to ensure that they do not take on tasks before they are ready or try advanced techniques before they are strong enough in the fundamentals. Likewise, young lawyers learn how to interview witnesses as a foundation for interviewing clients, as a foundation for taking a discovery deposition, and as a foundation for doing a direct examination.

Someone in the organization must care enough to look at the work that young lawyers are getting, to determine whether it suits the lawyer in his or her stage of development. In this model each lawyer learns what they need from the supervisor immediately ahead of them in the firm development. The task of supervision starts early in the lawyer's career: It cannot wait for the lawyer's yearly evaluation or until after the lawyer reaches partnership. Otherwise, the young lawyer's development will be haphazard and, at times, it will become a source of embarrassment to the firm. Yearly evaluations allow the associate to fail during the year, and mentoring provides the means to monitor, teach, and evaluate the associate along the way. There is nothing worse for the reputation of a firm than for a lawyer to be conducting a deposition, arguing a motion, or drafting a key provision in contract and not know what he is doing. It seems obvious that a mentor for each associate would be the best learning structure for a law firm.

> In its purest sense, mentoring is teaching, helping young attorneys, by example or by giving counsel. But good mentors do more than train novices in the art of lawyering. They act as advocates, significantly influencing a young attorney's career.[42]

Many firms and businesses agree that mentoring is a valuable tool in the development of associates: 60 percent of companies on the Fortune list of the "100 Best Places to Work" in 2002 had mentoring programs.[43] While mentoring programs are generally thought to be effective and beneficial, creating a successful program is difficult.[44] What does it take to be a good mentor? How should a program be structured?" While not clear, consensus exists on what makes a mentoring program a success. Examples of what works and tips on issues to consider are helpful in determining what program will best suit your firm or business.

In determining what it means to be a mentor, Elaine Fox describes three categories of mentoring. She explains that to be successful as a mentor, one must satisfy all three categories.[45] The first category of mentoring is the mentor as teacher, an informal professional who aids a young attorney by teaching him the ins and outs of the profession. Second, the mentor should serve as a sponsor, a connector who helps the young lawyer make necessary connections along her career path. The third category is the mentor as a person, one who manages the heart and spirit of the relationship, providing personal as well as professional assistance.[46]

Moreover, Fox notes that it is important to remember that the best lawyers are not necessarily the best mentors. Mentoring is a different skill than practicing, so think carefully when selecting a mentor or deciding to serve as one. Fox believes that the best mentor is usually someone who is a good person first and a good lawyer second.[47] Put simply, "being a mentor means really knowing your mentee, taking the time to be involved in his or her life, learning to listen, and letting your mentee sometimes set the agenda for your discussions."[48]

In NITA's Supervisory Skills program, most participants name mentors (though not necessarily in their firm or in the practice of law) who have been important in reaching the success they have reached. The common characteristics of mentors are described as follows:

- Willing to take the time to teach mentees, not only about the practice but about issues of personal growth and development
- Teach excellent skills
- Stress client service
- Teach and demonstrate integrity

- Instill faith in mentee
- Open to discussion of broader issues: firm politics, family, finding meaning and fulfillment in work, morality, philosophy, art, community service
- Teach strategies for not only preventing mistakes but for correcting mistakes after they are made
- Demonstrate loyalty, care, and compassion
- Take the blame for failings and give credit for success
- Instill confidence
- Take risks and turn over responsibility for important client matters
- Bring mentees along to client meetings

FORMAL MENTORING

Formal mentoring involves the existence of a structured program run by the firm or business in which "mentors maintain an ongoing dialogue with associates regarding their goals, what it will take to achieve those goals, and how the firm can support them."[49] While some debate the value of these formal programs, one source found that most associates said they would benefit from a more formal mentor program with an abundance of communication and clearly articulated expressions for the mentor-mentee relationship.[50]

When creating a formal mentoring program, consider the following guidelines:[51]

1. Make involvement time limited. If the program goes on too long, the focus will become diffuse and success will be hard to demonstrate.
2. Provide a system for feedback and evaluation. Allow mentees to provide information on whether the program is successful or not, so that the program can be evaluated and changed in response to these comments.
3. Develop clear goals. Unless goals are identified and reasonably precise, no one will know whether or not the mentor program is successful. Goals should be both clear and realistic.
4. Maintain confidentiality. During a mentor program, revealing comments are likely to be made by a mentee to a mentor. The mentee must be confident that these comments will remain only between the mentor and mentee; otherwise, the program will be either short-lived or internally censored by the mentee.
5. Maintain accountability. Power in the program ultimately rests with the mentors, so they should also bear responsibility for the program's success. If the mentee isn't meeting the program's goals, consider the responsibility of the mentor.
6. Make a contract. To ensure the relationship is as clear as possible, create a contract that sets out the expectations of both parties. Terms might include how much time is expected to be given by each and when.

Tips for Mentors[52]

Do	*Don't*
• Engage in the mentoring relationship prepared to exert energy, and, from time to time, even to experience frustration. • Make yourself available at identifiable times and for briefer, impromptu questions. • Accord due respect and confidentiality.	• Expect the mentee to adopt your precise style or comport themselves in the very shadow of your image. • Frustrate yourself by being unavailable or inaccessible, or amnesic about how hard the practice of law in the early years truly is. • Avoid the harder questions requiring judgment, but do avoid being judgmental. • Give up. Even if your efforts don't show tangible or consistent results, remember that mentoring is a long-term process and an important act.

Tips for Mentees[53]

Do	*Don't*
• Be mindful of your mentor's schedule. • Take initiative. Your mentor is likely to be as busy or busier than you are. • Express gratitude for your mentor's involvement and energies on your behalf. • Your part to develop the relationship, so that your mentor will trust you and embrace his or her role in your career.	• Schedule a mentoring meeting and fail to show up on time. • Take offense if your mentor has to cancel a session or is a bit difficult to reach from time to time. • Take for granted how hard it is for most lawyers to mentor others. • Quarrel with the advice your mentor provides—listen well and reach across your differences to accept the guidance you sought and need.

INFORMAL MENTORING

While a number of firms have formal mentoring programs, many do not. This does not mean, however, that one cannot go out on his or her own and find someone to serve in a mentor capacity.

If a firm wants to encourage informal mentoring, it should communicate to its associates how they might initiate such a relationship. A firm might send a memo suggesting the associate consider the following:[54]

- Be proactive about finding a mentor. Don't expect one to find you, and don't assume that the one to whom you were assigned will satisfy all of your needs.
- Define your needs. Be clear about the skills, contacts, or advice that you want.
- Look for mutual outside interests that will help cement the personal aspects of your relationship with your mentor.
- Don't try to mirror yourself in your mentor search. Look for someone who has different skills and approaches to things.
- Don't ask for an over-commitment of time and effort from a mentor. Be specific about what you need in the short-term and build the relationship over time.
- Build in reciprocal value. Show your respect and appreciation, work hard, and provide input and contacts that will benefit your mentor.

In any setting, it is important to build strong working relationships. To reach this end, the following tips are worthy of mention:[55]

- Don't wait for a mentor to be formally assigned to you. Proactively seek out people you respect and with whom you have things in common.
- Respect the time you spend with mentors and su-

pervisors. Be prepared to meet with them and don't overstep time boundaries.

- Respond promptly to phone messages and e-mails from supervising lawyers and others. Communicate regularly about the status of your projects and other efforts.
- Become an avid listener and observer to better understand others' needs and perspectives. Find opportunities to offer something in return.
- Be a mentor to others. It will help you to hone your leadership skills and allow you to give back to others.
- Earn and build trust, respect, and credibility with colleagues by being reliable, timely, accessible, and responsive.

REVERSE MENTORING

Reverse mentoring, while relatively new, is quickly becoming an essential tool in many firms and businesses. The idea is that the junior associate might have something to offer the more experienced lawyer. The junior mentors the senior. Reverse mentoring has occurred informally for years as younger associates have worked beside their elders, but formalizing and structuring of such relationships has been taking place recently. In 1999, now-retired CEO of General Electric Corp., Jack Welch, started the first formal reverse mentoring program. While no law firms have been specifically identified as having formal reverse-mentoring programs, various large corporations have such programs, including General Motors,

Deloitte & Touche, and Procter & Gamble. Some consultants suggest that reverse mentoring should be structured, with set times for meeting, specific goals, and a set duration. However, others note that, as with all successful mentoring teams, the relationship cannot be forced and participants must be compatible.[56]

In particular, firms need to realize that the new graduate may come armed with skills not held by the experienced lawyers in the practice. Recent graduates may have more knowledge and skill with regard to technology: for instance, knowledge and skill with computer hardware and software, computer and Internet research techniques, meta data, Web site creation and searching, all forms of digital data communication, presentation software, and business environments surrounding these matters. They may have special learning from law school or graduate school that makes their knowledge cutting edge in a specialty area. More and more law-school graduates have dual degrees, come with master's degrees or Ph.Ds, or degrees in medicine, nursing, business, and/or arts and architecture. They are often experienced travelers or have developed special interests in foreign culture and history. In sum, if a law practice can open itself up, the learning can occur both ways: both up and down the experience ladder.

CURRENT TRENDS IN LAW-FIRM MENTORING

Law firms across the country believe in the importance of mentoring, and many have created unique, strategic plans to make these programs succeed. By reviewing what is working for these firms, one is better able to create a mentoring program in his or her own firm.

One common thread among many firms is the existence of a professional development director. The job of the professional development director is to nurture lawyers beyond law school and to supervise the training of newer attorneys. In some cases, firms created these new positions from scratch, while other firms grew the positions over time, often designating a lawyer who gradually transitioned out of practice into firm management.[57] For example, Burton N. Lipshie, managing attorney for litigation at Stroock & Stroock & Lavan, is in charge of the development and training of the firm's new lawyers. His activities range from having weekly lunches with new associates to implementing formal training programs.[58] Other firms that have appointed directors of professional development to supervise the training of newer attorneys—in some cases full time—include: Dorsey & Whitney in Minneapolis; Foley & Lardner in Milwaukee; Hale & Dorr in Boston; Hughes Luce in Dallas; Lane Powell Spears & Lubersky in Seattle; Shearman & Stearling in New York; Shook, Hardy & Bacon in Kansas City; and Vedder, Price, Kaufman & Kammholz in Chicago.[59]

Another common approach is for a firm to put a current partner in charge of associate training. For example, Jones Day in Chicago appointed a partner to be in charge of firm-wide training and a partner in charge of litigation training in each office.[60] Likewise, Gibson, Dunn & Crutcher appointed a training partner in each office to administer a firm-wide training curriculum.[61] Going one step further, Stoel Rives in Portland, Oregon, appointed one of its experienced partners to be an associate coach, working one-on-one with associates, attending depositions and hearings that they conduct, and providing feedback and mentoring.[62] In a similar initiative, known at King & Spaulding as the Link Program, each new lawyer is paired up with a more senior associate and partner. The more seasoned associate, the "link host," often answers basic questions, such as what clothing is appropriate for casual Fridays.[63] Feedback on the program cites a valuable aspect of the program as the "ability to have someone to go to and ask dumb questions."[64]

Other firms tailor their programs to certain groups within the firm. For example, O'Melveny & Myers's New York office instituted a series of training sessions specifically addressed toward developing women's trial skills.[65] In this program, women attorneys view and discuss an ABA Section of Litigation Woman Advocate Committee video entitled *The Best of Both Worlds: Strategies for Balancing the Home Court and the Trial Court,* in which judges and practitioners share the strategies that have helped them balance work and parenting.[66]

Firms are also cognizant of the need to train mentors and review the program for areas that can be improved. In Dallas, Thompson & Knight requires partner mentors to attend a training program on how to be a better mentor.[67] Similarly, Banner & Witcoff of Chicago established an education committee within firm management to review annually the success of its in-house training and mentoring programs.[68]

Finally, various firms also use awards and other recognition programs to aid in the success of their mentoring programs. For example, Fenwick & West dubbed 2000 the "Year of the Mentor" in an effort to underscore the importance of mentoring skills.[69] In addition, the firm provides strong incentives for its partners to become effective mentors and provides mentoring training for its partners and senior lawyers throughout the year. Finally, the firm rewards good mentors with significant year-end bonuses.[70] Fenwick & West chair Davidson says the program is win-win for the firm because the partners develop new skills and its associates reap the benefits.[71] Similarly, Dorsey & Whitney of Minneapolis bestows annual Partner-of-the-Year awards to commend leadership in training and mentoring.[72]

While no clear strategy exists for how to implement and run a successful mentoring program, it is obvious that many firms across the country are coming up with interesting and unique ways to try to get a step ahead of the competition. Whether a formal or informal program works best in your situation, the benefits available from any program seem well worth the effort. On the other hand, mentoring is dependent on the interest and effort of the mentor and mentee. It cannot be forced upon either. In addition, time constraints in the practice of law make it increasing difficult for partners to take the time to mentor and for junior associates to have the time to learn. And when one has the time, the other often does not. Are there any strategies that a learning organization can implement that will develop important goals in environments where time and resources do not allow for the development of the more ideal mentoring relationships?

Still, the trade-off between the senior's billing rate and the junior's effectiveness and efficiency may be a close call on a firm-wide basis and ultimately work against a firm-wide mentoring effort. In addition, some supervisors are just not very good teachers. They are not interested in teaching and lack the social skills that would make them effective. If the time burden of mentoring is not shared equally in the firm, the senior supervisors can start to see mentoring as a lazy way out for some of his or her colleagues. They may even be slightly jealous or resentful of the friendships formed between mentors and mentees, preferring the "tough taskmaster" approach they experienced when they came up through the firm. If the firm does not value the time spent mentoring and treats it as unproductive time, the senior lawyers will conclude that it is simply better to let a survival-of-the-fittest mentality weed out those who go and those who stay.

· CHAPTER SEVEN ·

Leading from Behind

What we call leadership consists mainly of knowing how to follow. The wise leader stays in the background and facilitates other people's process. The greatest things the leader does go largely unnoticed. Because the leader does not push or shape or manipulate, there is no resentment or resistance.

—JOHN HEIDER, *The Tao of Leadership*, at 131

Law firms, not unlike many other organizations, often fail to choose as leaders those who are in fact most talented for that special role. For example, because of their traditional hierarchical structure, law firms will sometimes chose as leaders those who have been with the organization longest. Seniority does not itself make a leader. As we discussed earlier, often lawyers who have been practicing for many years have become the "unconscious competent": they are no longer interested in learning or teaching and may have little patience with the mundane aspects of the practice of law. These lawyers rarely make good leaders because they are not willing to listen hard and confirm understanding before launching in with their own questions and time-worn assumptions. An equally troubling error may befall a law firm that chooses its leaders based primarily on the relentless need to maintain or increase profits. Although many rainmakers may also be talented leaders, many are not. These lawyers have a talent at developing and keeping client work, but often that talent stems from, and is coupled with, an ego that interferes with leadership. In adapting Lao Tzu's *Tao Te Ching* specifically to address issues of leadership in today's business world, John Heider observes that the wise leader "keeps egocentricity in check and by doing so becomes even more effective."[73] Many law-firm rainmakers cannot readily accomplish keeping egocentricity in check.

Perhaps even more so for law firms than for other organizations, the functioning of the group is maximized when its leaders "lead from behind." Law firms generally consist of talented, hard-driving, independent thinkers who have self-selected private practice over government work because they want to have more control to shape their own destiny, to make their own decisions and their own mistakes, and to take full credit (and full blame). They are self-starters and bristle at excessive control. Leading a collection of such individuals has often been likened to "herding cats": each has her own view and had better be allowed to state it and to pursue it. Therefore, a leader of such a group is not likely to meet with success by imposing control, which surely will engender resentment and resistance. A skillful leader of such strong-willed and talented lawyers does well to focus on providing "opportunities, not obligations."[74]

Opportunities are created by a leader who listens ardently and keeps at questions until understanding is confirmed. A leader who speaks clearly and specifically lets her colleagues learn from their own words, often juxtaposing them and adding little or no commentary. The skills that allow for effective delegation and feedback, taken to a higher level, are the same that facilitate leading from behind.

CONCLUSION

Lawyers need to pay attention not only to supervisory skills and mentoring skills but also to leadership skills. I have learned from the lawyers whom I have taught management and leadership skills to over the past ten years that the need is certainly there. Lawyers in these courses are hungry for information about how to develop ownership of their work and maturity and in judgment—the ability to look at the big picture as well as the immediate task, to teach supervisees how to exercise good judgment, and to give wise, considered advice.

While teaching legal strategy, NITA faculty have been asked to explain how to best develop a criteria of strategic decision making that produces not only excellent client service but a shared language of the best ethical decision making. We've discussed how to measure litigation strategy against leadership principles: peace first, lowest cost, simplest to execute, least public exposure. While teaching our Advanced Negotiation and Mediation programs, we've been asked to teach how to resist becoming overwedded to a case, avoid losing by winning, and how to develop techniques to keep from becoming angry and reactive. There is a hunger in these courses for discussions and understanding of the stuff of leadership: of leading from a strong sense of self and priorities, of maturity, of how to develop a shared language of mission, of leading as partners and leading from behind—not from ahead or on top of junior employees.

A recent remark from a managing partner at a major New York law firm sums up the sentiments of many of these NITA program participants:

> If a law firm such as ours cannot develop an ethos that we are about more than making money, then we simply can not keep the best and brightest at our firm. Frankly, our associates can make more money applying their considerable intellectual skills and talents in other areas than at a law firm. We need to create a learning organization that seeks to develop leaders and expert problem solvers, in the best sense of these words, if we will be able to provide a place where our associates and partners can find meaning and fulfillment.

More and more firms are taking on leadership training and development as part of their programs in professional development. Some hire a psychologist to help them identify and assess leadership skills and strategies while others have sent their senior associates to courses at Wharton. Other major firms have tried to develop leadership courses and curricula for their internal use.

What is true for the big firms is true for lawyers from all walks of practice and who work in all size of firms. If a lawyer's aim is to simply make the most money, he or she can often do that in other ways than practice law. What makes the lawyer stay with the profession are the professional aspects of what she does, that is: to problem solve, offer wise advise, at times battle zealously, and at times act as a peace maker, and strive to make a difference in the lives of her clients to the end that justice is served and society is better off for it.

The lessons to be learned are to have a strong sense of the higher self, to manage your time to keep your priorities straight, to listen first and seek understanding before seeking power, to keep control and the advantage. These lessons also involve letting junior lawyers explore different styles and strategies for developing ownership of work, and stress a focus on excellent client service and the development of a shared language of purpose and mission.

It is also important to take the time to talk and reflect on leadership. This involves the development and use of simulations and role-playing that place new lawyers into situations that require leadership skills. Senior lawyers also need to provide feedback and facilitate discussion of approaches and skills that can lead to repeatable behaviors of excellent leadership. In the process, the leader provides others in the profession with a much needed bridge into the language of leadership and a way of initiating an important dialogue about what matters most in the practice of law.

NOTES

1. ABA Section of Legal Education and Admissions to the Bar, ABA, Teaching and Learning Professionalism 5 (1996).

2. *Id.* at 31–32.

3. Deborah L. Rhode, *Institutionalizing Ethics,* 44 Case W. Res. L. Rev. 665, 710–711 (1994).

4. The American Lawyer, *Two More Billion-Dollar Firms,* Am. Law., May 2006, at 145-46, available at http://www.law.com/jsp/tal/PubArticleTAL.jsp?hubtype=Cover+Story&id=1145803851957. In 2005, seven Am Law 100 firms broke the $1 billion gross revenue mark. Two firms are new to the billion-dollar club—Weil, Gotshal & Manges and White & Case. This year, for the first time, Latham & Watkins has surpassed Baker & McKenzie for the number two spot. Baker has ranked first or second on the gross revenue charts since 1988. The firm first posted revenue over $1 billion in 2001. Gross revenue figures on this chart are rounded to the nearest $500,000. Firms that tied in the rankings are listed alphabetically. Some firms provided fractional full-time equivalent or full-year equivalent lawyer numbers, which were rounded up to the nearest whole number. Firms marked with an asterisk have more than one partnership tier or some partners who are predominantly on fixed-income status.

5. Marc Galanter & Thomas Paylay, Tournament of Lawyers: The Transformation of the Big Law Firm 3-27 (University of Chicago Press 1991). This chart is made by taking data from Marc S. Galanter & Thomas M. Palay, *Why the*

Big Get Bigger: The Promotion-to-Partner Tournament and the Growth of Large Law Firms, 76 VA. L. REV. 747, 755–56 (1990) and adding 2006 data from each firm's web pages.

6. Robert L. Nelson, *Of Tournaments and Transformations: Explaining the Growth of Large Law Firms,* 1992 Wisc. L. Rev. 733, 737 (1992) (reviewing Marc Galanter & Thomas Palay, *Tournament of Lawyers: The Transformation of the Big Law Firm* (1991) (hereinafter Galanter & Palay); Marc S. Galanter & Thomas M. Palay, *Why the Big Get Bigger: The Promotion-to-Partner Tournament and the Growth of Large Law Firms,* 76 Va. L. Rev. 747, 755–56 (1990).

7. Robert L. Nelson, *Of Tournaments and Transformations: Explaining the Growth of Large Law Firms,* 1992 WISC. L. REV. 733, 737 (footnotes omitted) (1992) (book review).

8. *See* Raul O. Rodriguez, Mark T. Green & Malcolm James Ree, *Leading Generation X: Do the Old Rules Apply?,* JOURNAL OF LEADERSHIP & ORGANIZATIONAL STUDIES, Spring 2003, at 67; WORKFORCE TRENDS (Data Dome, Inc., Atlanta, Ga.), vol. 3, iss. 2, (2004), available at http://www.datadome.com/worktrends/worktrends3_2.pdf.

9. GALANTER & PALAY, *supra* note 6, at 77–120; Marc S. Galanter & Thomas M. Palay, *Why the Big Get Bigger: The Promotion-to-Partner Tournament and the Growth of Large Law Firms,* 76 VA. L. REV. 747, 755–56 (1990).

10. PETER M. SENGE, THE FIFTH DISCIPLINE: THE ART & PRACTICE OF THE LEARNING ORGANIZATION (Doubleday/Currency, rev. ed. 2006) (1990).

11. Senge writes that in 1983, a Royal Dutch/Shell survey found that one-third of the firms in the Fortune 500 as of 1970 have vanished. Senge hypothesizes that the problem for a business seeking to serve customers is that it must be able to adapt to a continually changing environment. *Id.* at 18. One way to accomplish this is to develop in employees a discipline

that attempts to achieve for each individual a sense of personal mastery. *Id.* at 147.

12. *Id.* Senge calls this "overcoming the basic diseases of the hierarchy." *Id* at 181.

13. *See* Rodriguez, Green & James, *supra* note 8 (describing the literature on the transient nature of Generation Xers and their preferences for flexibility, harmonious work environment, and fulfillment in their work.) The authors conclude:

> Xers preferred a challenging task accomplished within a workday. Boomers preferred a challenging task accomplished in several days. What Generation X wants from their leaders in order to feel fulfilled at work may be different from the needs of boomers. Xers preferred surfing and buying/using the Internet while boomers preferred using the telephone. Boomers preferred regularly scheduled hours. Xers preferred flexible hours. It is fair to say that while boomers expect to work regularly scheduled hours, they may find themselves working longer hours than they desire. Boomers preferred a job that provided a retirement plan with benefits. Xers preferred a portable 401K with lump sum distribution.
>
> The differences in individual preferences for leadership behavior may require a shift in leadership attitude, policy, and implementation. Most of the baby boomers are currently retiring or considering retiring in the near future. Although it is apparent that Xers have different work environment preferences, it will be interesting to see if leadership behavior will change to accommodate this paradigm shift. This study provided an insight into the preferences for leadership behavior of the young and older employees in a working environment. Relatively little is known about Generation X and leadership. The

recognition of Generation X preferences may help managements determine the type of leadership behavior needed to guide and inspire its workforce. *Id.* at 74-5

See also The Journal of Leadership Studies, which is available on loan from the OSU Leadership Center. A complete listing of all the Leadership Center's resources is available on its Web site at http://leadershipcenter.osu.edu.

14. Although we will speak in terms of law firms, all of the suggestions in this section apply in all practice settings. The devices utilized in large law firms to effectively supervise and train junior lawyers are equally applicable in law firms of all sizes, not-for-profit agencies, and governmental practice settings.

15. Professor Douglass Blaze and Professor Michael Johnson, Gaining Expertise, (unpublished manuscript) University of Tennessee, (2006)(on file with author) [hereinafter, Gaining Expertise]; *See also* K. Anders Ericsson, *The Acquisition of Expert Performance: An Introduction to Some of the Issues, in* THE ROAD TO EXCELLENCE: THE ACQUISITION OF EXPERT PERFORMANCE IN THE ARTS AND SCIENCES, SPORTS, AND GAMES 1-50 (K. Anders Ericsson ed., Erlbaum 1996).

Professor Ericsson is the expert on gaining expertise. Other more recent publications by Ericsson on the subject include: K. Anders Ericsson, *Attaining Excellence Through Deliberate Practice: Insights from the Study of Expert Performance, in* THE PURSUIT OF EXCELLENCE IN EDUCATION 21-55 (Michael Ferrari, ed., Erlbaum 2002); K. Anders Ericsson, *Development of Elite Performance and Deliberate Practice: An Update from the Perspective of the Expert Performance Approach, in* EXPERT PERFORMANCE IN SPORTS: RECENT ADVANCES IN RESEARCH ON SPORT EXPERTISE 49-81 (Janet L. Starkes & K. Anders Ericsson eds., Human Kinetics 2003); K. Anders Ericsson, *How the Expert Performance*

Approach Differs from Traditional Approaches to Expertise in Sports: In Search of a Shared Theoretical Framework for Studying Expert Performance, in EXPERT PERFORMANCE IN SPORTS: RECENT ADVANCES IN RESEARCH ON SPORT EXPERTISE 371-401 (Janet L. Starkes & K. Anders Ericsson, Human Kinetics 2003); K. Anders Ericsson, *The Acquisition of Expert Performance as Problem Solving: Construction and Modification of Mediating Mechanisms Through Deliberate Practice, in* THE PSYCHOLOGY OF PROBLEM SOLVING 31-83 (Janet E. Davidson & Robert J. Sternberg eds., Cambridge University Press 2003); K. Anders Ericsson, *The Search for General Abilities and Basic Capacities: Theoretical Implications from the Modifiability and Complexity of Mechanisms Mediating Expert Performance, in* THE PSYCHOLOGY OF ABILITIES, COMPETENCIES, AND EXPERTISE 93-125 (Robert J. Sternberg & Elena L. Grigorenko eds., Cambridge University Press 2003); K. Anders Ericsson, *Deliberate practice and the acquisition and maintenance of expert performance in medicine and related domains,* 79 ACAD. MED. 10, S1-S12, (2004).

16. Gaining Expertise, *supra* note 15.

17. I first learned about learning stages in relationship to firms in seminars and conversations with Maude Pervere, who first learned of these ideas from teaching and work done by Tony Roffers. Tony Roffers, PhD, is a licensed psychologist with a private psychotherapy practice in Oakland, California. He has served on the faculty at the University of California (U.C.), Berkeley; San Francisco State University; Saint Mary's College of California; and Stanford University. Dr. Roffers consults with a wide variety of professional organizations and gives guest lectures in the law schools at U.C., Berkeley; Stanford University; U.C., Davis; and Hastings. Dr. Roffers has taught communication skills workshops for groups of practicing attorneys throughout Northern California, including the U.S. Ninth Circuit Court of Appeals in San Francisco, the

Collaborative Law Group in San Francisco, the Northern California Mediation Association, the American Association of Matrimonial Lawyers (AAML), the Alternative Dispute Resolution Sections of the Sonoma Bar Association and the Seattle Bar Association, and JAMS/Endispute in San Francisco. He has also led empathy training and conflict resolution workshops for the National Institute for Trail Advocacy (NITA).

18. Dr. Tony Roffers, address at seminar on firm and leadership development (1990). *See supra* text accompanying note 17.

19. This listening technique is transferable into a variety of practice settings. It helps diffuse anger and deadlock in a negotiation setting, where a lawyer demonstrates an ability to listen and reflect the other side's position before putting forth a solution of her own. The expert mediator also knows this technique as a way to facilitate both catharsis and as a bridge to more creative problem solving.

20. Steven Lubet, Modern Trial Advocacy: Analysis and Practice (NITA 3d ed. 2004).

21. David M. Malone, Peter T. Hoffman & Anthony J. Bocchino, Effective Deposition: Techniques and Strategies That Work (NITA 3d ed. 2006).

22. Anthony J. Bocchino & Paul J. Zwier, Fact Investigation: A Practical Guide to Interviewing, Counseling, and Case Theory Development (NITA 2000).

23. David M. Malone & Paul J. Zwier, Effective Expert Testimony (NITA 2d ed. 2006).

24. Thomas F. Guernsey & Paul J. Zwier, Advanced Negotiation and Mediation Theory and Practice: A Realistic Integrated Approach (NITA 2d ed. 2005).

25. Paul J. Zwier, Legal Strategy (NITA 2005).

26. Deanne C. Siemer, Frank D. Rothschild & Paul J. Zwier, Teaching Legal Strategy (NITA 2006).

27. Stephen V. Armstrong & Timothy P. Terrell, Thinking Like a Writer: A Lawyer's Guide to Effective Writing and Editing (Practicing Law Institute 2d ed. 2003).

28. David Ball, On Damages 76 (NITA 2001).

29. NITA Teaching Supervisory Skills Vignettes.

30. Stephen V. Armstrong & Timothy P. Terrell, Thinking Like a Writer: A Lawyer's Guide to Effective Writing and Editing 305–307 (Practising Law Institute, 2d ed. 2003).

31. Adapted from Armstrong & Terrell, *id.* at 311.

32. *Id.* at 16–17.

33. *Id.*

34. *Id.* at 299.

35. Steven R. Covey, Principle-Centered Leadership 270 (Free Press 1990).

36. What follows adapted from Paul J. Zwier & Anthony J. Bocchino, Fact Investigation: A Practical Guide to Interviewing, Counseling, and Case Theory Development 50-66 (NITA 2000).

37. Example comes from Robert P. Burns & Steven Lubet, Problems and Cases in Trial Advocacy Vol. I: Cases Problem 1, Investigator Bier (NITA CLE Rev. 5th ed. 1992).

38. Joel Brinkley & Steve Lohr, U.S. v. Microsoft: The Inside Story of the Landmark Case 138 (McGraw-Hill 2001) (describing John Warden's strategy to apply arguments he made in an earlier Kodak case where the court allowed "innovation" to trump "tying" product restrictions in anti-trust litigation).

39. *Id.* at ch. 3.

40. This technique was first taught to the author by Maude Pervere and later modified by Sandra Johnson.

41. Patrick Lencioni, The Five Dysfunctions of a Team: A Leadership Fable (Jossey-Bass 2002).

42. Hope Viner Samborn, *The Buddy System—More Than*

Just a Retention Tool, Mentoring Builds Relationships, A.B.A. J., Sept. 2000, at 86.

43. Susan Raridon Lambreth & Kelly A. Fox, *Making Your Firm a Great Place to Work,* L. PRAC. MGMT., May/June 2002, at 49.

44. *Id.*

45. Elaine S. Fox, *Aspects of Lawyer Mentoring,* PROF. LAW., Nov. 1995, at 16.

46. *See id.*

47. *See id.*

48. Patricia Lee Refo, *Training the Next Generation of Lawyers: Perhaps Our Greatest Challenge,* LITIG., Summer 2003, at 4.

49. *See* Virginia Grant & Marci M. Krufka, *The Young and the Restless,* L. PRAC. MGMT., Jul./Aug. 2004, at 48.

50. *See id.*

51. George Kaufman, *Everyday Mentoring,* L. PRAC. MGMT., Oct. 2000, at 60.

52. *See* Kathy Morris, *C'Mon You Can Do It,* BUS. L. TODAY, July/Aug. 1999, at 29.

53. *See id.*

54. *See* Susan Saltonstall Duncan, *Building Strong Mentor Relationships,* LAW PRAC. MGMT., Jan./Feb. 2004, at 49.

55. *See* Susan Saltonstall Duncan, *Freshout,* LAW PRAC. MGMT., Mar. 2003, at 43.

56. *See id.*

57. *See* Merrilyn Astin Tarlton, *Getting Invested in Professional Development,* LAW PRAC. MGMT., Oct. 2003, at 8.

58. *See id.*

59. *See* ABA Section of Litigation, Report of the Task Force on Training the Trial Lawyer (June 2003), http://www.abanet.org/litigation/taskforces/training/ttlreport.pdf.

60. *See id.*

61. *See id.*

62. *See id.*

63. *See* Stephanie Francis Ward, *Coming of Age: When It Comes to Mentoring, Younger Is Sometimes Better,* A.B.A. J., Jan. 2004, at 27.

64. *See id.*

65. *See* ABA Section of Litigation, *supra* note 62.

66. *See id.*

67. *See id.*

68. *See id.*

69. Lambreth & Fox, *supra* note 46.

70. *Id.*

71. *Id.*

72. *See* ABA Section of Litigation, *supra* note 62.

73. John Heider, The Tao of Leadership: Lao Tzu's Tao Te Ching Adapted for a New Age 13 (Humanics Publishing Group) (1992).

74. *Id.* at 135.

ABOUT THE AUTHOR

Paul J. Zwier is a professor at Emory University School of Law where he directs the trial advocacy and litigation skills programs and also teaches torts and advanced negotiation, mediation, and international law seminars. He is the director of public programs for the National Institute for Trial Advocacy and specializes in designing learning-by-doing programming for teaching advanced legal skills.

He has taught supervisory skills and leadership courses more than fifty times at more than twenty different law firms and legal organizations over the last ten years. He has taught courses in advocacy, litigation skills, and ADR at more than 250 law firms and legal organizations in the United States, and internationally in Africa, Canada, China, England, Guam, Ireland, Scotland, and Siapan. He also consults on ADR strategies as well as case theory and presentation in trial cases.

Other NITA Books by Paul J. Zwier

Effective Expert Testimony 2d ed. (NITA, 2006) (with David M. Malone)

PowerPoint for Professors (NITA, 2006) (with Deanne C. Siemer & Frank D. Rothschild)

Legal Strategy (NITA, 2005)

Advanced Negotiation and Mediation Theory and Practice: A Realistic Integrated Approach (NITA, 2005) (with Thomas F. Guernsey)

Fact Investigation: Interviewing, Case Analysis, and Counseling for Effective Representation (NITA, 2000) (with Anthony J. Bocchino)

Expert Rules (NITA, 1999) (with David M. Malone)